Behind Beavis And Butt-Head

A division of Shapolsky Publishers, Inc.

Behind Beavis and Butt-Head

S.P.I. BOOKS
A division of Shapolsky Publishers, Inc.

Copyright © 1994 by I. E. Mozeson

All rights reserved under International and Pan American Copyright Conventions. Published in the U.S.A. by Shapolsky Publishers, Inc. No parts of this book may be used or reproduced in any matter whatsoever without written permission of Shapolsky Publishers, Inc., except in the case of brief quotations embodied in critical articles or reviews.

ISBN 1-1-56171-306-6

For any additional information, contact:

S.P.I. BOOKS/Shapolsky Publishers, Inc.
136 West 22nd Street
New York, NY 10011
212/633-2022 / FAX 212/633-2123

Printed in Canada

10 9 8 7 6 5 4 3 2 1

Contents

INTRODUCTION

CHAPTER ONE
Why The Beavis And Butt-Head Show Is So Popular 14

> STUDENTS RESPOND TO THE QUESTION:
> "WHY DO YOU THINK THE BEAVIS AND BUTT-HEAD SHOW IS SO POPULAR?"

CHAPTER TWO
The Show's Image Of Teenage Boys 35

> STUDENTS RESPOND TO THE QUESTION:
> "WHAT IS THE SHOW'S IMAGE OF TEENAGE BOYS? IS IT AN ACCURATE ONE?

CHAPTER THREE
Beavis And Butt-Head's Values 53

> STUDENTS RESPOND TO THE QUESTION:
> WHAT ARE BEAVIS AND BUTT-HEAD'S VALUES? DO YOU SHARE INTEREST IN THE THINGS THEY LIKE TO DO?

CHAPTER FOUR
Responsibility For The Actions Of Viewers ... 71

> STUDENTS RESPOND TO CRITICISM AGAINST THE BEAVIS AND BUTT-HEAD SHOW

CHAPTER FIVE
Beavis And Butt-Head When They Grow Up 93

> STUDENTS DESCRIBE WHAT THEY SEE BEAVIS AND BUTT-HEAD DOING IN THE FUTURE

CHAPTER SIX
The Best Beavis And Butt-Head Jokes 113

> WHAT ARE YOUR FAVORITE BEAVIS AND BUTT-HEAD JOKES CIRCULATING AROUND YOUR SCHOOL?
> BEAVIS AND BUTT-HEAD'S FAMILY 115
> OUT-TAKES FROM BEAVIS AND BUTT-HEAD'S HISTORIC MEETING WITH PRESIDENT CLINTON 117
> BEAVIS AND BUTT-HEAD AT LARGE 120
> BEAVIS AND BUTT-HEAD ON SEXUALITY 129

CHAPTER SEVEN 132
The Media's Reaction To Beavis and Butt-Head

> THE EVOLUTION OF A MEDIA PHENOMENON
> AN ANALYSIS AND A SYNOPSIS OF THE MOST INTERESTING BEAVIS AND BUTT-HEAD COMMENTS THAT HAVE BEEN INUNDATING THE MEDIA.

Dedicated to my family

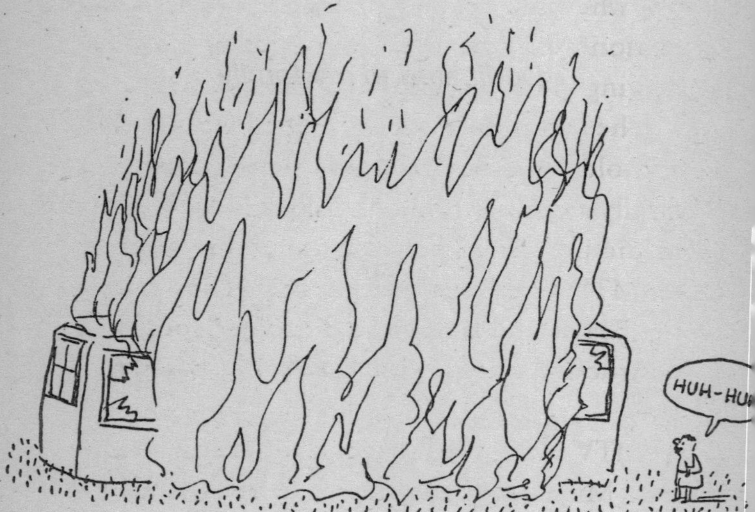
HUH-HU

INTRODUCTION

Beavis and Butt-Head are everywhere in our face. Controversy follows them more devotedly than their millions of MTV fans. Serious columnists in the newsweeklies, not just the entertainment writers, were trying to figure out just why these crudely drawn unanimated animation dudes are so damn popular — and unnerving to both parents and the establishment.

The media Butt-Mania peaked when a five-year-old Ohio boy tragically burned down his family's mobile home, killing his little sister in the process. The grieving mother went after MTV, blaming the death on her son watching Beavis and Butt-Head do some "cool" and destructive things with their only passion — fire.

MTV and the creator of the cartoon characters, Mike Judge took the heat for this fire — but you be the judge. Who are the real Butt-Heads here? Is TV responsible for inspiring acts of senseless violence or are parents too negligent with their latch-key, boob tubed vidiot kids?

This fire-starter was far too young to be watching MTV or to have access to a cigarette lighter. The king of anti-censorship for media, radio personality Howard Stern, blamed this tragedy squarely on the absentee parent. And if watching cartoons can be blamed for violence, then all the Tom and Jerry, Roadrunner, Flinstones and other cartoons containing violence certainly have to be considered for removal from the air. Must we cancel all versions of Superman because some child somewhere is bound to launch himself off a rooftop wearing a red cape?

I viewed many episodes of Beavis and Butt-Head myself, but I knew that the only way to see why the show was so popular and how kids really related to it was to ask Beavis and Butt-Heads' peers.

With my contacts in the public schools and area colleges I set about recording some Beavis and Butt-Head episodes on videocassettes, writing up a brief questionnaire, and giving the cassettes and "homework" assignments to English classes at several different schools. The teachers involved liked the "lesson plan", but they did have principals, deans and careers to

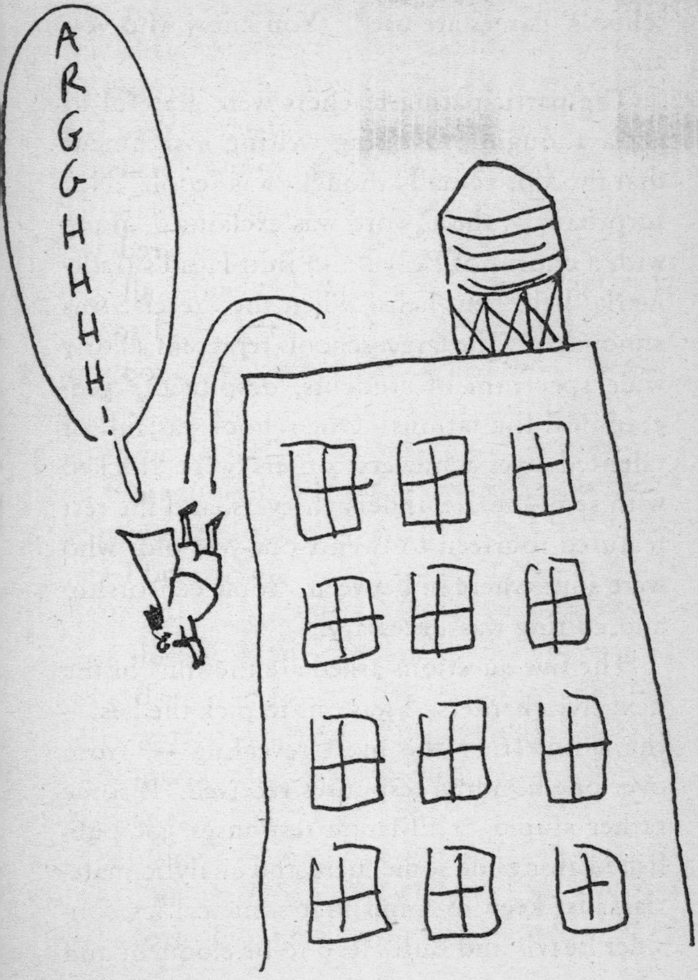
ARGGHHHH!

think about. (Censorship sucks.) But, to put everyone at ease, no identifiable students' or schools' names are used. (You know who you are.)

The participating teachers were grateful to get a thought-provoking writing assignment that the kids actually thought was "cool." Not surprisingly, the C-word was exclaimed, along with a chorus of Beavis and Butt-Head's trademark "heh, heh, hehs" when the exercise was announced. The target schools represent a fairly wide spectrum of students, despite the geographical limitations. One school was full of talented over-achievers, others were stocked with semi-literate under-achievers, and the rest featured fourteen to twenty-one-year-olds who were somewhere in between. Some censorship and editing was necessary.

The five questions asked are the stuff of the next five chapters. I was out to pick the best — the funniest or the most revealing — from over one hundred responses received. If some rather stupid or illiterate responses got published alongside some lucid and analytic material, just keep in mind that some critics consider Beavis and Butt-Head to be eloquent and

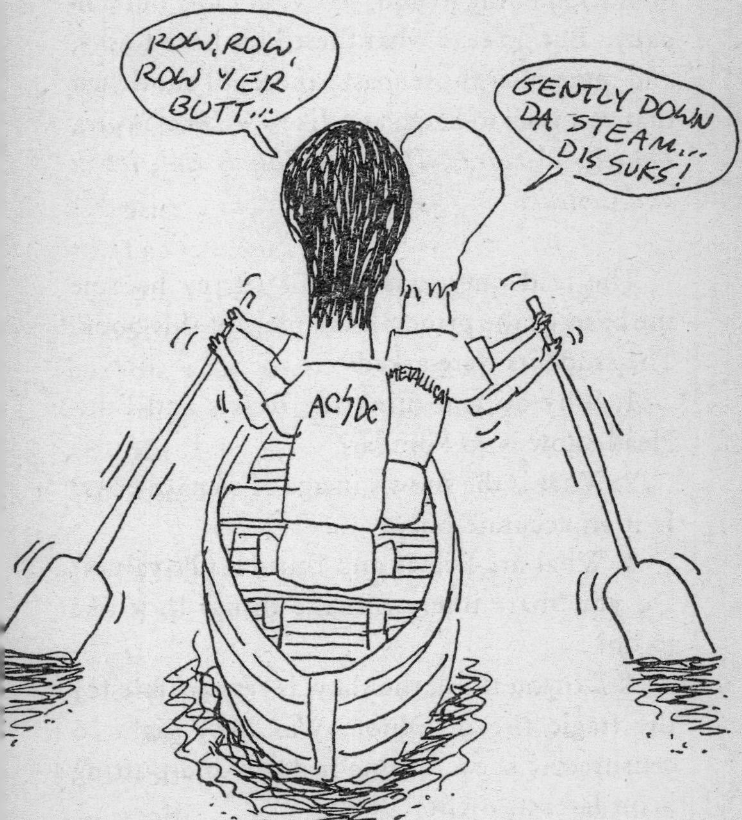
ROW, ROW, ROW YER BUTT...
GENTLY DOWN DA STEAM... DIS SUKS!
AC/DC
METALLICA

profound. If you are under thirty you are more culturally equipped to enjoy Mike Judge's MTV craft with *Beavis and Butt-Head*. If the whole Beavis and Butt-Head sensibility is foreign or even frightening to you, you've got lots of company. But do read what these kids have to say, and remember those masterpieces of subtle wit that you used to laugh at — like *The Three Stooges, Laurel* and *Hardy, The Little Rascals and Abbott and Costello!*

The lead questions in this survey became the basis of the principle chapters of this book. The students were asked:

1. Why do you think the Beavis and Butt-Head show is so Popular?

2. What is the show's image of teenage boys? Is it an accurate one?

3. What are Beavis and Butt-Head's values? Do you share interest in the things they like to do?

4. Do you think the show is responsible for the tragic fire in Ohio? Was MTV right to censure the show, toning it down and putting it on later at night?

5. Sketch a picture of what you see Beavis

and Butt-Head doing in the future...perhaps working at a job as professional critics, advertising writers or salesmen.

6. Many Beavis and Butt-Head jokes are circulating around the schools. What are your favorites?

CHAPTER ONE
Why The Beavis And Butt-Head Show Is So Popular

Students respond to the question: "Why do you think the Beavis and Butt-Head show is so popular?"

Students respond to the question: "Why do you think the Beavis and Butt-Head show is so popular?"

Response:

"Beavis and Butt-Head are two fine young men who are truly in touch with themselves. But sometimes they've got to stop touching themselves!."

— *Gary F.*

"Beavis and Butt-Head are popular as row [sic] models."

— *Lamont W.*

"These guys are, uh, cool, because they are not afraid to, you know, espress themselves."

— *Maria L.*

"I don't watch T.V. Who are Beaver and Buffcoat?"

— *Dipti G.*

"I watched the videos, okay. You want me to write about it now? Forget about it! Words suck."

— *Drew K.*

"The show is popular because it's a cartoon. Kids are programmed to stare at anything in a cartoon. It doesn't matter if it's got talking roadrunners or Tasmanian devils. If it's a cartoon we'll watch it. My little brothers and sisters don't get the jokes in 'The Simpsons' or 'Ren & Stimpy' either — but they'll watch these shows like they are revelation from Jesus Christ."

— *Angela F.*

"This is MTV's top rated show?! It just proves that it's the teeny boppers, between eleven and fifteen, who watch all the videos and buy most of the cd's and tapes. No wonder the music industry sucks!"

— *Stephen K.*

"The look is very different from any other show. This is refreshing.

(continued)

B&B Class Humor

Why did Beavis get kicked out of English class?

💣 Because he started laughing when the teacher said, "Don't use BUT to start a sentence."

Instead of the usual clever dialogue in all the sit coms, these dorks hardly get a sentence out. But they have lots to say if you think about it."

— *Pauline S.*

"It makes us laugh at ourselves. We all know butt-heads like them in real life."

— *Marion A.*

"If *Beavis and Butt-Head* was a turd, it would, like, be the same thing."

— *Ricky N.*

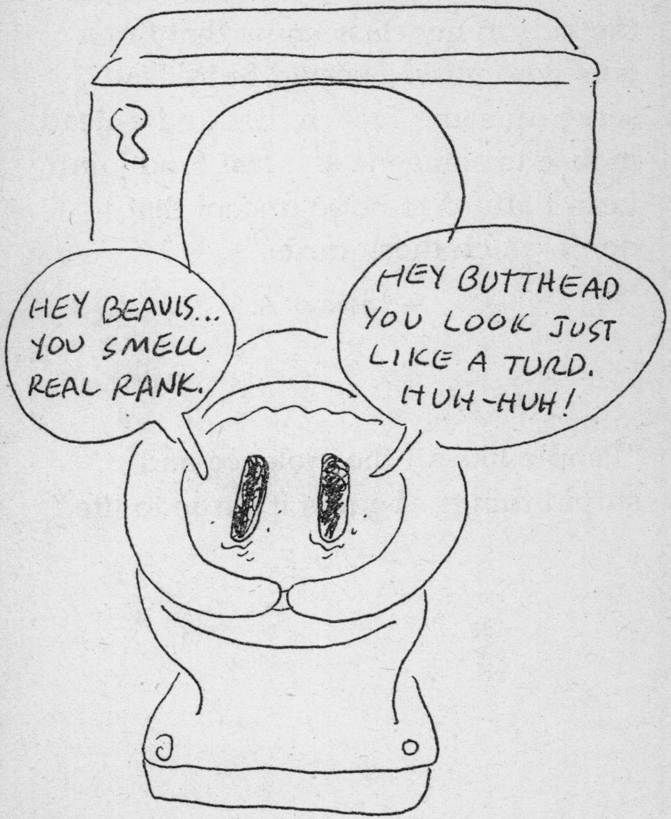
HEY BEAVIS... YOU SMELL REAL RANK.
HEY BUTTHEAD YOU LOOK JUST LIKE A TURD. HUH-HUH!

"To tell you the truth, I don't get why these dumb white butt-holes are so friggin' funny. But everybody watches it. What am I gonna do? Let the kids in my class know that I'm a wus who missed seeing Butt-Head serve up some French flies and a dead mouse to someone at a fast food joint? I can't afford to be so uncool that I don't watch those turds."

— *Lashawn A.*

"People like all the violence and stupid things. I guess it's true to life."

— *Ellen F.*

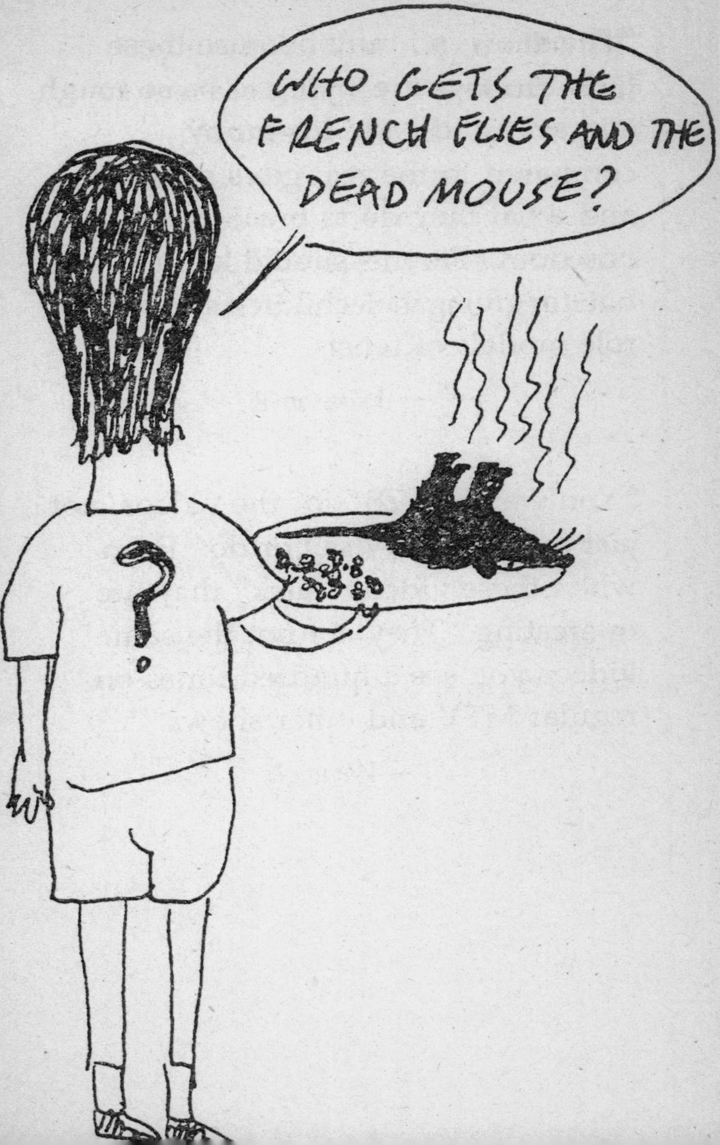
WHO GETS THE
FRENCH FLIES AND THE
DEAD MOUSE?

"The show is funny because these little dirtbags are trying to be so tough and sexy and bad. It's funny compared to the real guys out there and what they do to break the boredom. Parents should kiss MTV's butt for giving their children such mild role models of rebels.

— *Winston T.*

"You watch 'B&B' for the videos, not just for what they say or do. Even when these videos "suck" they are interesting. They are not the same videos you see a hundred times on regular MTV and other shows."

— *Wendy L.*

"They are two television people who are with a little mental illness. Viewers find joys in this."

– Kang N.

"Well, you have to laugh a little when you hear their stupid laugh all the time. It's just like all those stupid comedies on T.V. The laughter is fake, just a tape of audiences laughing. But it still makes you laugh at the sit coms when you hear all that fake laughter. "Ren & Stimpy" might be just as funny. But if I don't hear laughter I'm not sure when it's really being funny."

— *Jennifer W.*

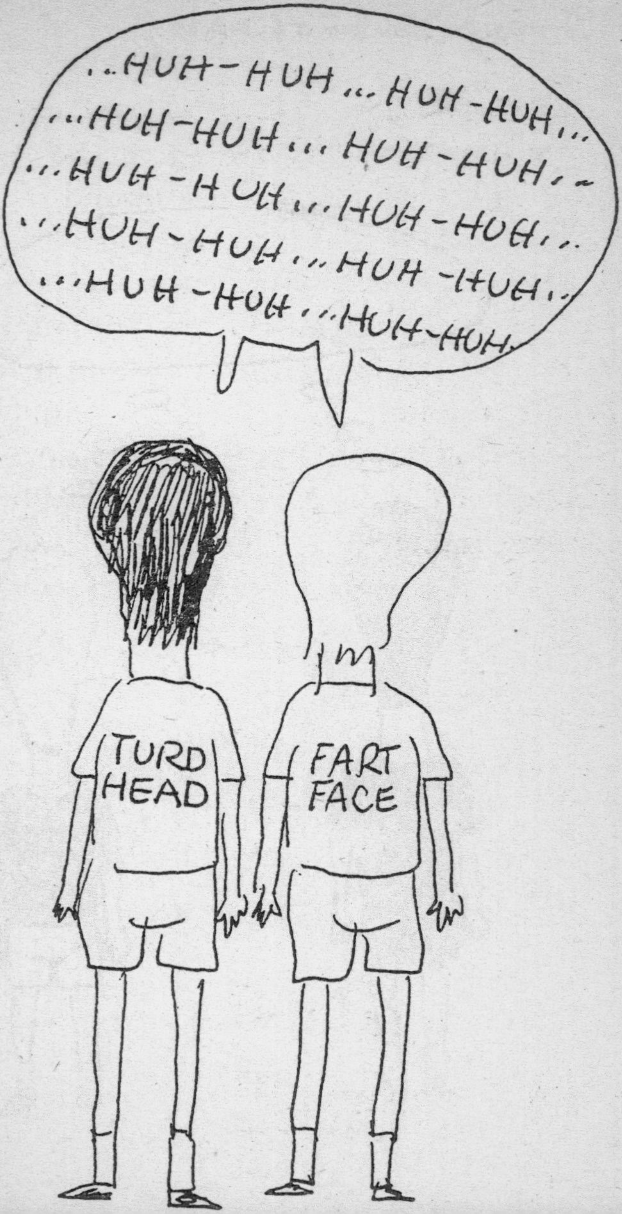
...HUH-HUH ... HUH-HUH... ...HUH-HUH... HUH-HUH... ...HUH-HUH... HUH-HUH... ...HUH-HUH... HUH-HUH... ...HUH-HUH... HUH-HUH
TURD HEAD
FART FACE

26 • Why The B&B Show Is So Popular?

"Being stupid is the power behind Beavis and Butt-Head. Only these guys are stupid enough to say everything on their mind.

— *Freddy C.*

(continued)

B&B Class Humor

Why did Butt-Head get kicked out of class when asked to discuss Iran's Ayatollah Khoemieni?

> 💣 Because he said the Ayatollah was up "Shiite's Creek."

"And what they say is funny. A lot of guys watching a music video might be thinking about how the musicians and models must be getting a lot of great sex. Beavis and Butt-Head come out and say these things."

— *Carmine D.*

"Beavis and Butt-Head make watching the videos more fun. During the rest of MTV programming you are not thinking about if the videos are good or bad. Even if MTV calls something the number one requested video, the chances are pretty good that you might hate it. At least we have these cartoon dudes coming right out and saying that many of these videos "suck."

— *Reggie L.*

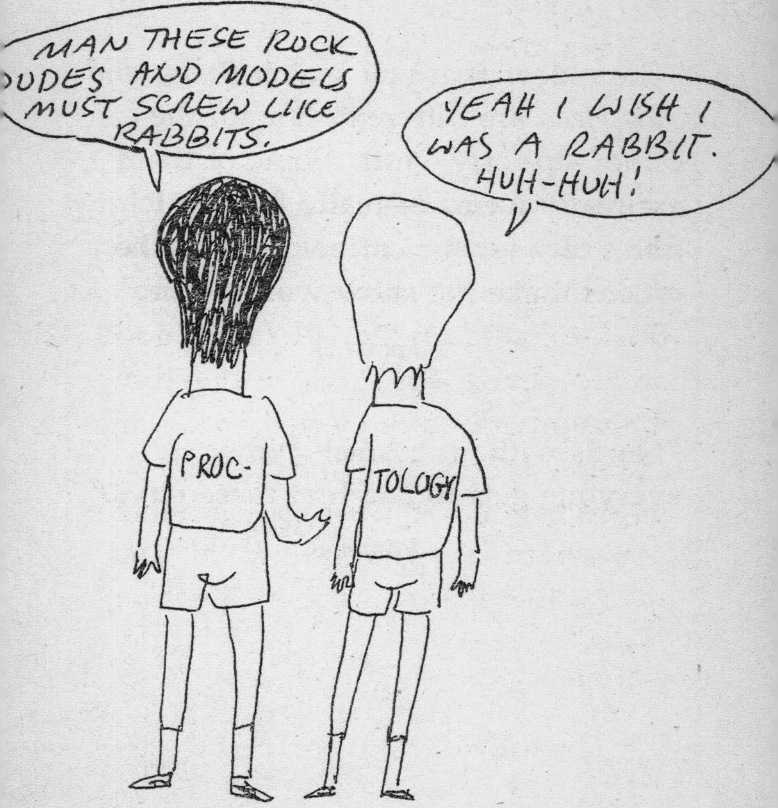
MAN THESE ROCK UDES AND MODELS MUST SCREW LIKE RABBITS.
YEAH I WISH I WAS A RABBIT. HUH-HUH!
PROC-
TOLOGY

"The show is popular because we see what we have in common with these guys — butts!"

— *Paula J.*

"The videos that you see on *Beavis and Butt-Head* are different. It's not the same 'top-forty' stuff. Some of them are really weird or really funny. I don't care for the cartoon at all. The videos make the show worthwhile."

— *Louise D.*

"Nerds without brains! Wow, everyone gets to laugh at these guys."

— *Wayne S.*

(continued)

B&B Class Humor

Why did Beavis get kicked out of current events class?

💣 Because he thought "Iran" was how an Iraqi described his war experience.

"Sorry, I don't have a clue why this show is popular. I only watch it when the other stations are showing golf tournaments and real estate seminars."

— *Nelson B.*

"I think it appeals to everyone who feels or felt the frustrations of being a thirteen-year-old kid. The hormones are raging, but the kids don't know why. Young Beavis and Butt-Heads are too stupid and ugly to have a relationship with a real girl. To me, that little laugh, "huh-huh," is sexual frustration. The violence, animal torture and all that is sublimated sexual aggression. I know. I'm a psych major."

— *Andrew C.*

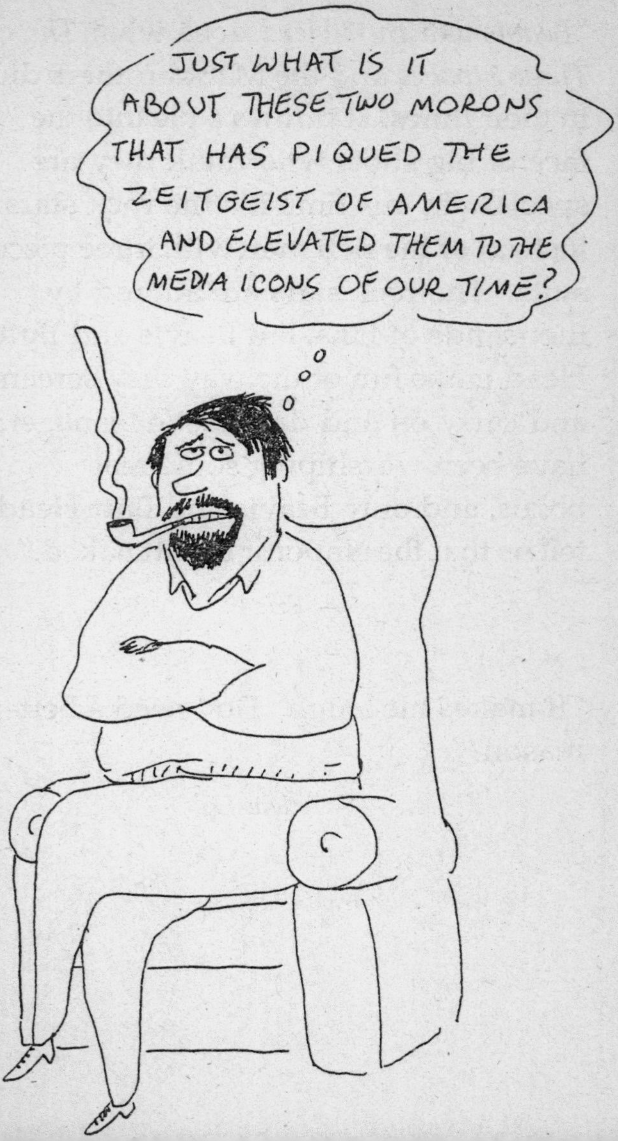
JUST WHAT IS IT ABOUT THESE TWO MORONS THAT HAS PIQUED THE ZEITGEIST OF AMERICA AND ELEVATED THEM TO THE MEDIA ICONS OF OUR TIME?

"*Beavis and Butt-Head* does what *The Three Stooges* and the Marx brothers did in their times. It throws a pie into the face of big shots who think they are special. In our time it's the rock stars instead of the rich men with three piece suits. The rock stars are adored by thousands of fans, but Beavis and Butt-Head make fun of the way they scream and carry on and dress. We teenagers have been worshiping some real bozos, and only Beavis and Butt-Head tell us that the emperor is butt naked."

— *Eric F.*

"It makes me laugh. Do I need a better reason?"

— *Arlene D.*

CHAPTER TWO
The Show's Image Of Teenage Boys

"WHAT IS THE SHOW'S IMAGE OF TEENAGE BOYS? IS IT AN ACCURATE ONE?"

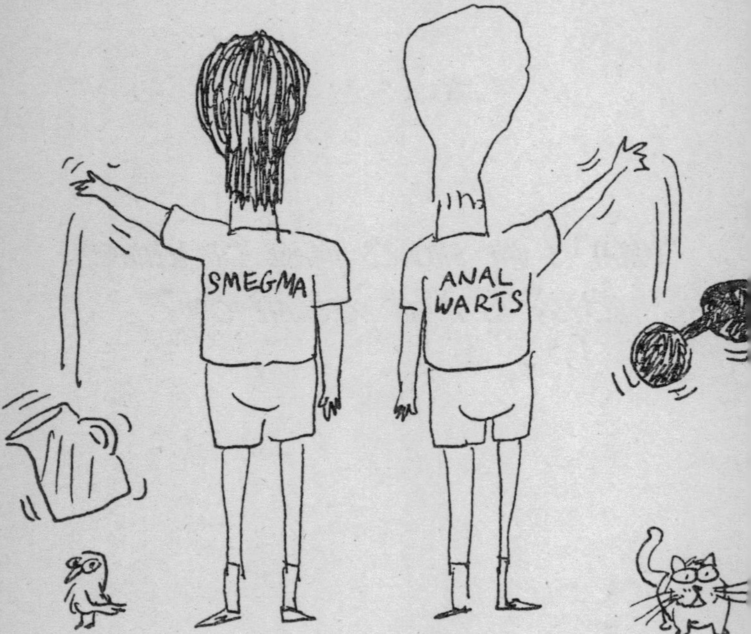
SMEGMA
ANAL WARTS

"WHAT IS THE SHOW'S IMAGE OF TEENAGE BOYS? IS IT AN ACCURATE ONE?

RESPONSE:

"I don't know anybody like Beavis and Butt-Head in real life. Well, nobody I would admit to knowing."

— *Ralph B.*

(continued)

B&B Class Humor

Why did Beavis get kicked out of Sunday school when asked to discuss Creation?

> 💣 Because he said, "On the Eighth Day, God took complaints."

"Beavis and Butt-Head are portrayed as a couple of Butt-munches. And you are what you eat."

— *Sandy L.*

"It's accurate because these pathetic wussies want to be big muscular dudes with facial hair, tatoos and bonable bitches. Beavis and Butt-Head watch these videos and call them 'cool' because they portray the fantasy they like. Videos that are artistic or new wave, with guys that are sensitive or creative are the ones that 'suck.' These videos don't feed their boyish macho fantasies."

— *Andrea N.*

"It's damn accurate. Being ugly, stupid, cruel and crude is what thirteen-year-old boys do best. This is the real world with Beavis, not like what's shown on *Leave It To Beaver*. You can't get ugly kids with braces to act on TV. That's why this had to be a cartoon."

— *Julian W.*

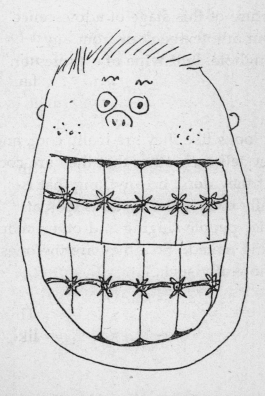

"Teenage boys are portrayed as sexist animals. And that is exactly what they are!"

— *Nicole D.*

"These two kids are totally anal retentive. You can't get a truer picture of this stage of adolescence from any textbook or from any bunghole, butt-wipe of a professor."

— *Art P.*

"It looks like they are really cool, and they tell each other that they are cool. But they don't do anything that is really cool. All they do is look at other people singing and other people being naked. So... they are the ones who really suck."

— *Mario H.*

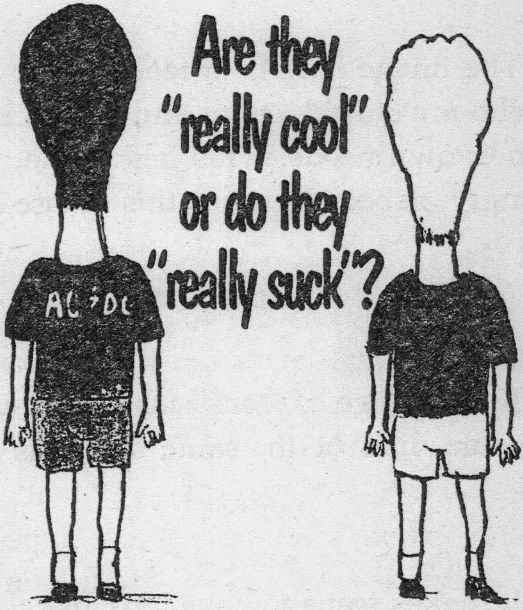
Are they
"really cool"
or do they
"really suck"?

"Of course everybody knows someone like Beavis and Butt-Head. That's everybody's sucky little brother!"

— *Rosalee G.*

"The image here is of teenager boys who are stupid, crazy and totally into their own needs. This makes me angry. Especially since this image is so true."

— *Marisol M.*

"If the image of teens was a turd, it would, like, be the same thing."

— *Ricky N.*

"It makes teenage boys look like Mongolian idiots who break the law and have no respect for man or beast. This is an utter distortion of reality —

and I'll rearrange your face if you disagree."

— *Vinny C.*

"Yes, it's pretty true. Teenage boys will do anything to get attention. Mostly bad things, of course."

Marla S.

"These wack toyboys ain't like the homeys in my posse. They like that heavy metal turd. They gotta kick the butt of frogs and cats because they sure as hell can't get busy on the street."

— *Scoobie D.*

"If Bart Simpson skateboarded onto their MTV show he would kick their asses. Bart is younger, but he's smarter and tougher than these two retards."

— *Greg K.*

"*The Brady Bunch* tries to be real and it's phoney. *Beavis and Butt-Head* tries to look very unrealistic but it's real."

— *Brenda A.*

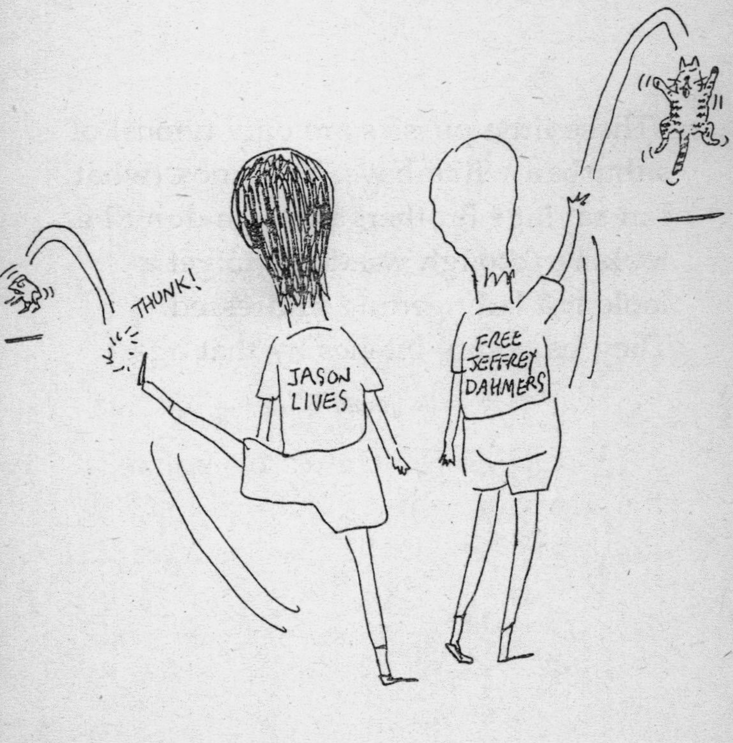
THUNK!
JASON LIVES
FREE JEFFREY DAHMERS

"That air guitar crap is pretty accurate. Most of the metal heads in my school are just as goofy. In real life these no-talent butt-wipes couldn't even play a harmonica in their butts after a bowl of baked beans."

— *Jeffery W.*

"These little pussies are only typical of suburban white boys. You know what I'm saying? Brothers that age don't be looking through windows to get a look at a lady getting undressed. They be bonin' bitches by that age."

— *Jamal B.*

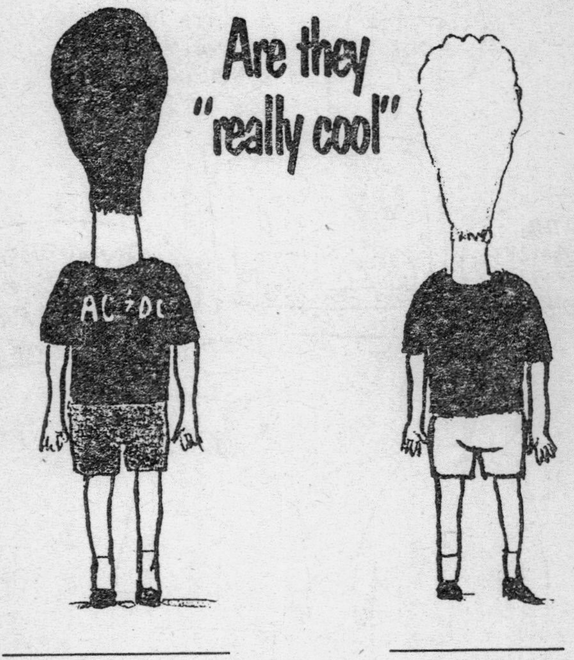
Are they
"really cool"
AC/DC

48 • The Show's Image Of Teenage Boys

"Western teenage boys are always insulting each other, being cruel, dirty and saying that everything different from them sucks. This is a very accurate picture, and the only program that shows this. I wish this program were shown in China. Then we wouldn't be sent here to live among such low people."

— *Huang C.*

"Beavis and Butt-Head are saying the same thing Michael Jackson says: 'I'm bad, I'm bad, you know it.' This is the typical song for teenagers in that rebelious stage — but Beavis and Butt-Head don't have Michael's talent. They sing terribly. They try to participate by watching others sing on videos."

— *Roberta A.*

"Teenage boys look like criminals. In my country they would be treated as criminals. Here they are called entertainers and crime is entertainment. The only crime in America is low ratings."

— *Amin B.*

"I asked my nine-year-old sister. She's the big B & B fan in the house. She says Beavis and Butt-Head are just like real kids my age. Am I being dissed here or what?"

— *Barry T.*

"Speaking of image, these boys aren't just ugly. They are repulsive. Bad hair, bad teeth, bad clothes. It seems obvious to me that we are supposed to laugh AT them, not WITH them."

— *Melena N.*

"Planet Beavis is a totally unreal world. There are never parents or family obligations. Even a dufus dad like Homer Simpson is better than no father at all. This isn't an accurate picture of life as a young person, but I guess it's attractive for many of the viewers."

— *Roger S.*

B&B Class Humor

Why did Butt-Head get kicked out of accounting class?

> 🌀 He thought bookkeeping was trying not to lose your books.

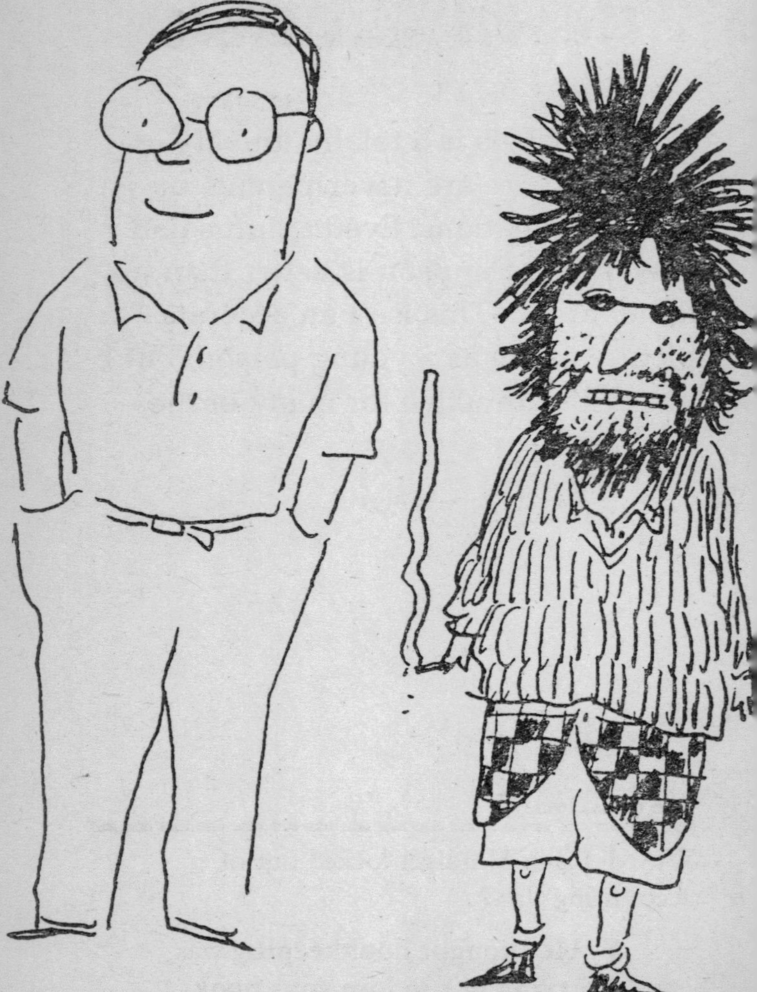

CHAPTER THREE
Beavis And Butt-Head's Values

WHAT ARE BEAVIS AND BUTT-HEAD'S VALUES? DO YOU SHARE INTEREST IN THE THINGS THEY LIKE TO DO?

Students respond to the question:

What are Beavis and Butt-Head's values? Do you share interest in the things they like to do?

Response:

"They believe in speaking out for stuff that's cool. They like stuff that's cool. I like stuff that's cool. That makes us cool. And another thing. We both don't like stuff that sucks. We share these values, like a common bond between us. Beavis and Butt-Head are our friends."

— Ernie W.

"Could you, uhm, repeat the question?"

— *Silvester S.*

"Beavis and Butt-Head share all-American values, enshrined in the Constitution of these United States. Long live the 'pursuit of happiness.' (Now all this doesn't mean that we are not a nation of idiots.)"

— *Benny G.*

"Beavis and Butt-Head are looking for self-esteem — in all the wrong places and all the wrong ways. And like the sisters sing, they are 'never gonna get it.'"

— *Yelitsa B.*

"You mean do I choke the chicken, spank the monkey, play pocket pool or shake the snake? Well, maybe if I'm watching a video that's got some naked chicks."

— *Hermano Pee Wee*

"They have a need to say everything sucks. They are trying to be cool, and the only way they can do it is by saying that everything else is no good."

— *Connie P.*

"Their values are all about bad haircuts, bad attitudes and great taste in videos."

— *Joey T.*

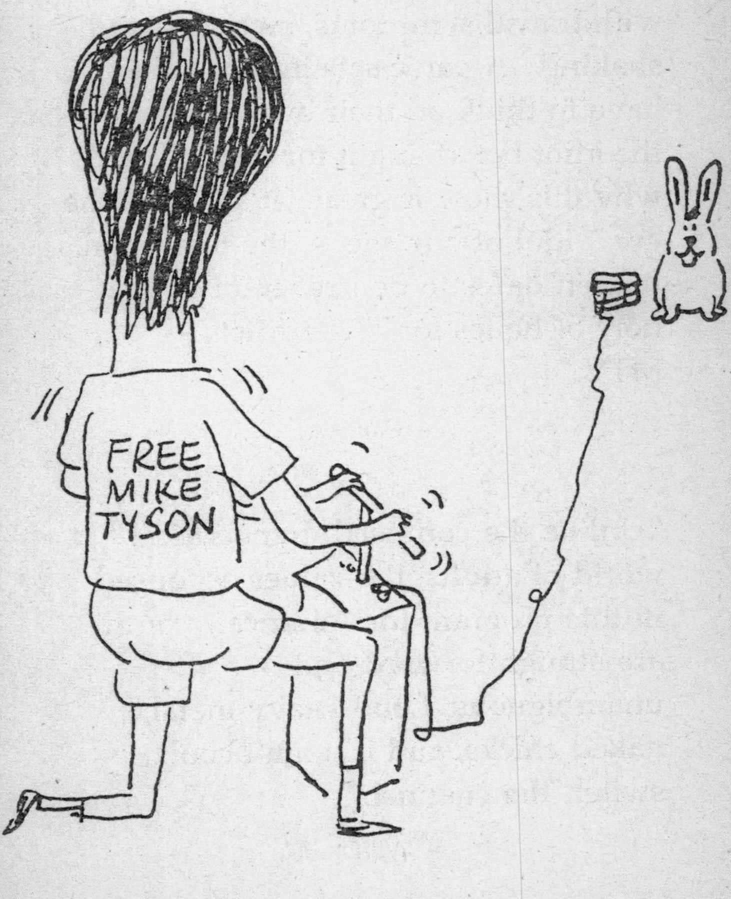
FREE
MIKE
TYSON

"I think Beavis and Butt-Head live for T.V. In the one episode where they are separated from this mind drug they go nuts. They have real withdrawal symptoms, sweating and shaking. A panic sets in when they have to think on their own instead of the idiot box doing it for them. That's why this show is great. It smashes the great idol of our age — the television. It even dares to be irreverent in the holy of holies for T.V. addicts — MTV."

— *Camille F.*

"Unlike the confused, hypocritical world of adults, the values espoused in this program for American youth are straightforward and unambiguous: Loud heavy metal, naked chicks, and if it ain't cool... switch the channel."

— *William M.*

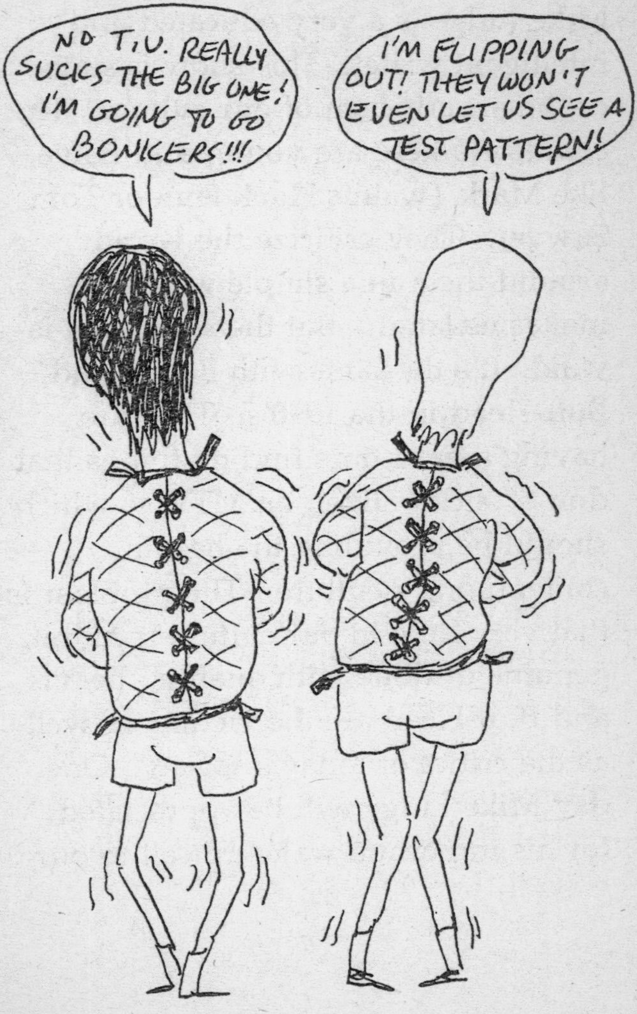
NO T.V. REALLY SUCKS THE BIG ONE! I'M GOING TO GO BONKERS!!!
I'M FLIPPING OUT! THEY WON'T EVEN LET US SEE A TEST PATTERN!

"Don't be fooled by the simple cartoon art or the simple dialogue. Mike Judge is a very educated and intelligent writer. This show is state-of-the-art criticism of our culture. The characters here are young and naive, like Mark Twain's Huck Finn or Tom Sawyer. They criticize the world around them in a simple way that makes us laugh. But their criticism is valid. It's the same with Beavis and Butt-Head in the 1990's. They are having a hard time finding things that don't "suck." Even on MTV — which should be providing the best in contemporary culture. The problem is that very little in our culture is moral, genuine or done with quality. Beavis and Butt-Head are the victims as well as the critics of today's society. One day Mike Judge will be appreciated for his important wake-up call to our loud, technically advanced but empty civilization.

— *Jerry H.*

"You got to agree with B & B. Most of life just sucks. Get me a remote so I can turn it off."

— *A Nonny Mouse*

"Their values are all about getting people's attention for doing the wrong thing. When anyone yells at them they just laugh because they are

(continued)

B&B Class Humor

Why was Butt-Head kicked out of history class?

> 💣 Because he thought the feminist movement was when a girl went to the bathroom.

finally getting the attention they want."

— *Marla S.*

"I don't know if the word 'values' counts for anything here. If it keeps Beavis and Butt-Head from being bored than its cool. If they are forced to think for a second it sucks."

— *Paul B.*

"You don't have to agree with Beavis and Butt-Head every time they criticize a video. The main thing is that they do it. We don't have to sit back and watch turd set to music and visuals. If it sucks, we can come out and say so. Or we can hit the remote, like our cartoon heroes do. I think B & B is all about choice and freedom. Isn't that what America is for?"

— *Melissa C.*

"The only value these couch potatoes have is TV. It's like the Simpsons who all run to the TV. The first TV shows to make fun of watching TV were *All in the Family* and then *Married With Children*. Instead of Archie Bunker or Al Bundy the passive males who try to dominate the TV (their whole world) are "sons" of Archie and Al — Beavis and Butt-Head. Of course this is funny, and we should be laughing at them — unless we, too, are too hypnotized by the TV to notice.

— *Warren S.*

(continued)

B&B Class Humor
───────────────────────────

Why was Beavis flunked out of art class?

> 💣* Because he wrote: "Pic-ass-o was a famous art dude with brown-fingers."

"Their values are not having any."

— *Annie H.*

"If their values were a turd, they would, like, be the same thing."

— *Ricky N.*

"Values? Uhm, is that like the money you pay for stuff when you can't shoplift it?"

— *Tony V.*

"One of the main reasons Beavis and Butt-Head put down some videos is because they are older and different from the narrow kind of heavy metal music that they like. Their values are bad because they cannot accept anything different."

— *Layla H.*

"Education, social contacts, true love — these are the great values that these peckerheads have never heard of."

— *Gary D.*

"These peckerheads don't have any values. They never work for anything. When they finally earned some money jerking off at a sperm bank they went out and bought porno magazines. So they could jerk off some more!"

— *Franklin L.*

"Having a good time is what matters to them. They only want to be entertained by videos they like and going on wacky adventures. Are these bad values? Everybody does the same thing in life. Beavis and Butt-Head just do more of it."

— *Pat H.*

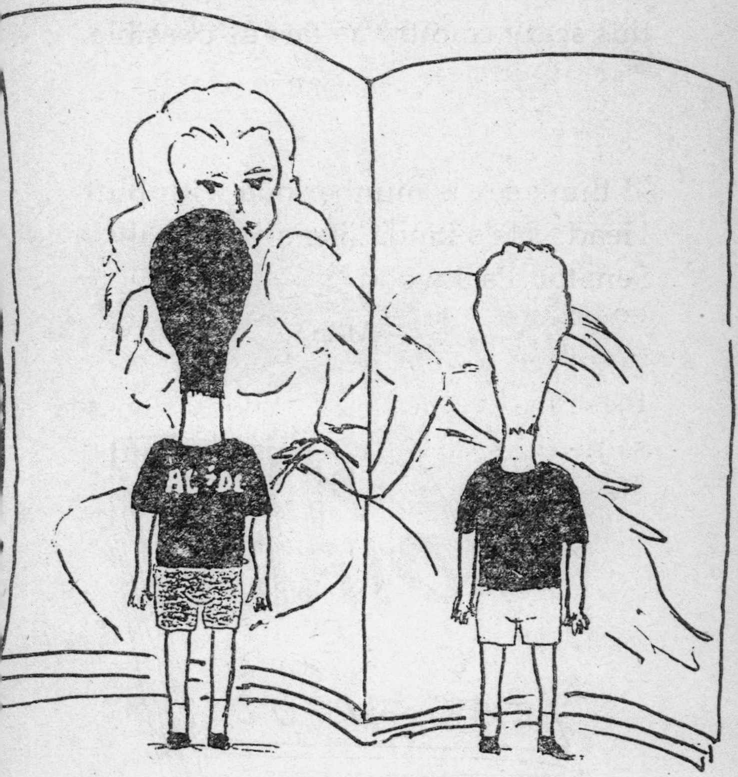
AC/DC

"I don't share a thing with these butt-faces. When I figure out what values American teenagers have I will let you know. Meanwhile, let me earn my million dollars quickly and get out of this scary country as fast as possible.

— *Amin B.*

"I think sex is number one with Butt-Head. He's kinda like a young Senator Packwood."

— *Mike S.*

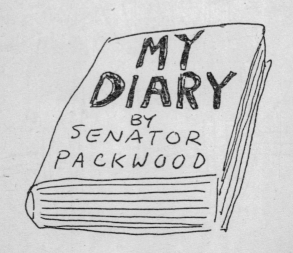

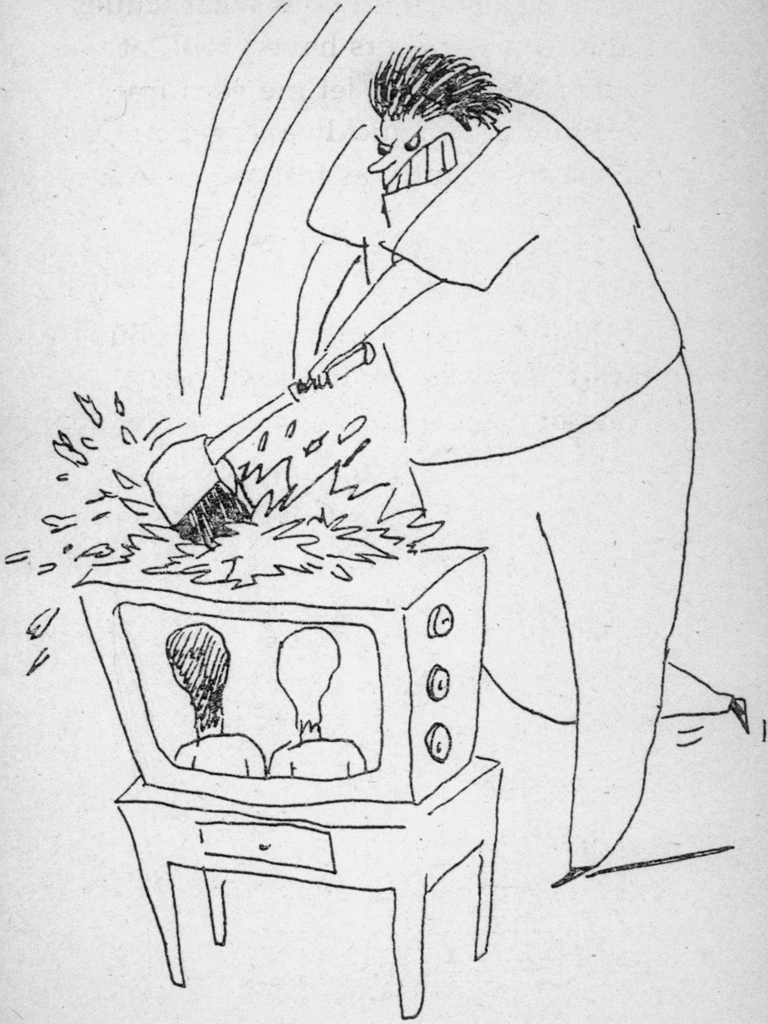

CHAPTER FOUR
Responsibility For The Actions Of Viewers

Students respond to criticism against the Beavis and Butt-Head show

Students Respond to Criticism Against the Beavis and Butt-Head Show

Response:

They are specifically asked if they think the show is responsible for the tragic fire in Ohio that killed a two-year-old girl when her brother lit a "cool" fire just like Beavis did. Was MTV right to censure the show and put it on later at night?

"Hey, I'm young, but I wasn't born yesterday. Before TV people murdered and raped too. Did anybody blame violent novels for that? Of course not! Now they are blaming TV just because more people watch it than read paperback horror novels."

— Stella T.

"Yes, the show is very dangerous for younger kids to watch. It's okay if people do bad things on T.V. and then get punished. Then it's a lesson in how to behave right instead of wrong. When Bart Simpson does something wrong he always pays the price. These creeps never catch hell for blowing up animals or destroying expensive things.

The message is to go ahead and kidnap children or sneak into nudist camp grounds. It's cool. You'll always get away with it. This is not a message for kids who don't know right from wrong."

— *Emily G.*

"Being afraid of censorship sucks. This is a cable TV show. Do you know what kind of language, sex and violence gets on cable all the time? Cable is not for kids, unless Mommy is there watching the Disney channel with you.

— *Patricia M.*

BEHIND BEAVIS AND BUTT-HEAD • 75

"Nobody forces you to choose one channel out of one hundred in this country. We can't let somebody tell us what we can and can't have on the media. Otherwise we'll have one government regulated station and a dictatorship. Achtung, Baby!"

— *Stan M.*

"Beavis and Butt-Head do a lot of things that my pastor would say is sinful. Especially the masturbation. But I can't say that this show can influence anybody to do bad things that are not already in their heart. If a normal boy has no religious training and he's got a joy-stick, what's to stop him from playing video games with himself? ... The one episode that did have religion in it had a phoney cult figure and references to televangelists who hire hookers. If they are going to

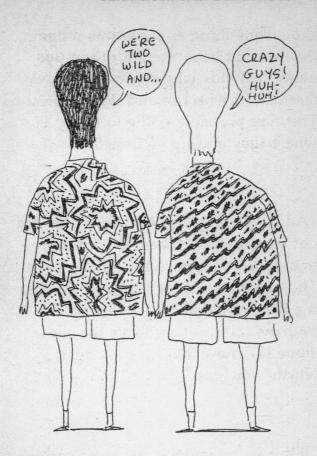

B&B Class Humor

Why were Beavis and Butt-Head thrown off every sports team?

💣 **They kept beating themselves.**

show something as serious as religion, they should be more fair. There are many real kids who share Beavis' fascination with fire and destruction. They are probably going to love where they end up — in hell!"

— *Christina G.*

"Adults just don't get it. And they are not supposed to. There is a lot more to censor at seven o'clock than *Beavis*. They are just picking on MTV because it's the only network for teenagers. Well, as soon as they leave the show alone I'll know that it's no longer worth watching."

— *Justin L.*

"If this kid copied the action of a cartoon character like Beavis, can you imagine what this Einstein would do if he saw *Terminator* or *Tales from the Crypt*?!"

— *Felix M.*

"This five-year-old was a troubled kid. We've got millions of them in this country. He was desperate to do something that would finally get his mother to pay attention to him — and not his sister. Unfortunately, Beavis was there to give him a "really cool" idea. If this boy were restricted to watching the right things for his age, like *Barney* or *Sesame Street*, he might have gotten his mother's attention with a cute song and dance."

— *Marla S.*

(continued)

B&B Class Humor

Why did the biology teacher tell Beavis and Butt-Head that they resembled a bloated large intestine?

> 💣* Because he was expecting those turds to get expelled any moment.

"I agree with Howard Stern. The MTV people are a bunch of wussies. They are supposed to be cool and hip and rebellious. B.S.! They are a bunch of scared preppies."

— *Manny A.*

"I know this isn't going to be popular, but I really think MTV had to get this show away from young children's eyes. Older kids know that Beavis and Butt-Head are butt-heads. But smaller kids just know that the show is fun. The explosions and fires are fun things, and they wish they could do them too. If they get a hold of their big brother's firecracker, you know they want to set it off. If they see a cool fire on their big brother's TV show, then they want to light one of those too."

— *Michelle Z.*

"This stuff is harmless. Just a Nineties version of *The Little Rascals* or *Dennis the Menace*. Do you know what real kids are doing in the streets of Harlem and Compton? These Butt-Head guys aren't going to smoke crack, catch AIDS from a homeless hooker or get raped in jail."

— *Maggie L.*

"Now the damn lawyers are messing with cable TV. MTV couldn't get sued for the first time a kid dies from a fire. But now that there was a big stink

(continued)

B&B Class Humor

Why did Beavis get kicked out of the same class when discussing Beethoven's last movement?

> 💣* Because he wondered why nobody flushed that old turd down the toilet.

about it...oh boy! They had to drop the fire stuff and change the time because some bastards are waiting to nail MTV for 50 million as soon as his kid dies from a Beavis fire. The second time ... after the warnings, they get you for gross negligence. There must be fifty alcoholic building supers in the South Bronx right now who are planning to clear their gambling debts and fly back to the islands with the money they figure to get from suing MTV. They are dragging boxes full of newspapers into their foster kids or step-kids' rooms and giving the kids lighters and matches to play with the second they hear the word 'fire'. "

— *Brandon V.*

"Of course they shouldn't care about stupid things that they are accused of. The show is trying to be real. Real

boys do these bad things. Are we
going to stop showing crime shows
because people weren't behaving
nicely?"

— *Sandra T.*

"That's right, blame the Messenger,
blame MTV for raising a generation of
buttfaces. Why make parents
responsible for parental supervision?
Who is in control in these homes?
These parents turn on the electronic
babysitter and just go away. If kids
were watching music videos without
the Beavis and Butt-Head what were
they getting? The same glorification
of violence, degrading of women and
disrespect for law."

— *Mary S.*

"M.T.V. did the right thing to move *Beavis and Butt-Head* to a later time and to tone down Beavis' pyromania. The show has too much of an influence over young kids. There are even Beavis and Butt-Head parties in Junior Highs. Nobody's house or cat is safe from kids who've just watched a *B & B* marathon."

— *Angel R.*

"If censorship was a turd, it would, like, be the same thing."

— *Ricky N.*

"If you don't think *Beavis and Butt-Head* can be a dangerous influence on dopey kids you've got to check out our cafeteria. How many guys are walking up to me with their goofy friends and saying things like: 'I think she wants me, huh-huh, huh-huh.'"

— *Yvette P.*

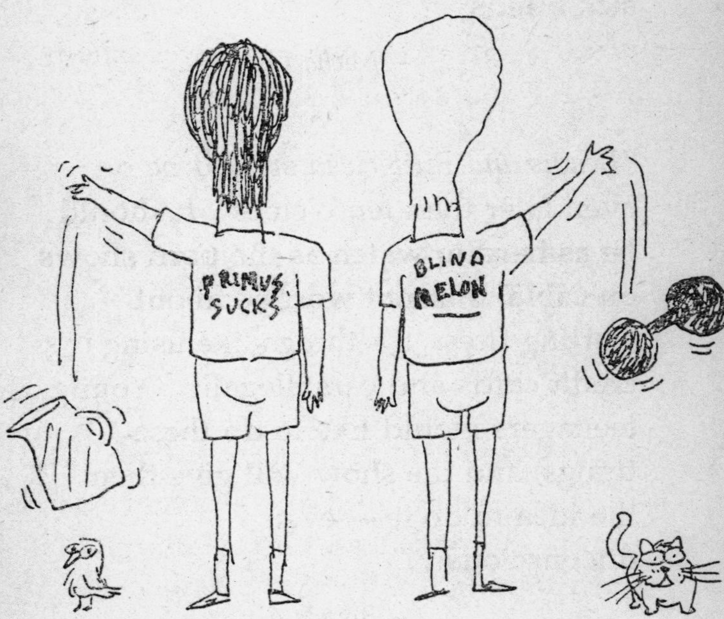
PRIMUS SUCKS
BLIND MELON

"This is really the same as the guns issue. What makes people kill, the guns or their brains? The answer is their brains. So what makes violent kids do violent things, TV or their brains? You guessed it — their own sick brains!"

— *Michael F.*

"*Beavis and Butt-Head* should be on even later than ten o'clock. It should be as hard to watch as the porn shows on cable. I'm not worried about starting fires. It's things like using credit cards and cars illegally. Young teenagers would like to do these things, and the show will give them the idea to do it — even unconsciously."

— *Brenda A.*

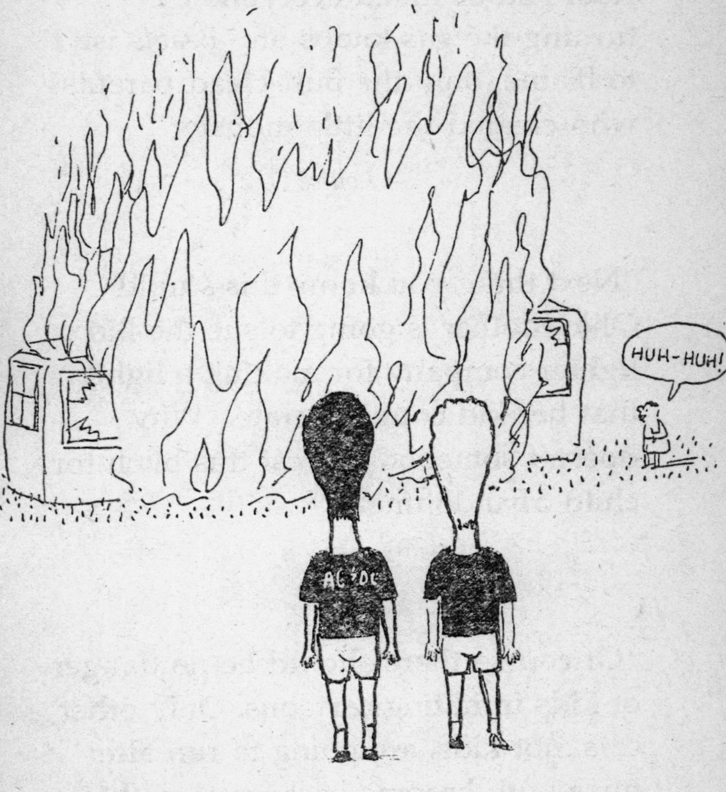
HUH-HUH!
AC/DC

"The kid who lit the fire was disturbed. If he didn't burn his house down he would have put Clorox in his Kool-Aid or killed everyone by turning the gas knobs on. *Beavis* isn't to blame, only the Butt-Head parents who created the little monster."

— *Louise D.*

"Next thing you know this stupid Ohio mother is going to sue the Bic lighter company for making a lighter that her kid could operate. Why doesn't somebody arrest this bitch for child abandonment?"

— *Alan F.*

"Of course there should be no danger of kids imitating cartoons. Only other cats, not kids, are going to run after mice with brooms because they 'hate those meeces to pieces.' But the

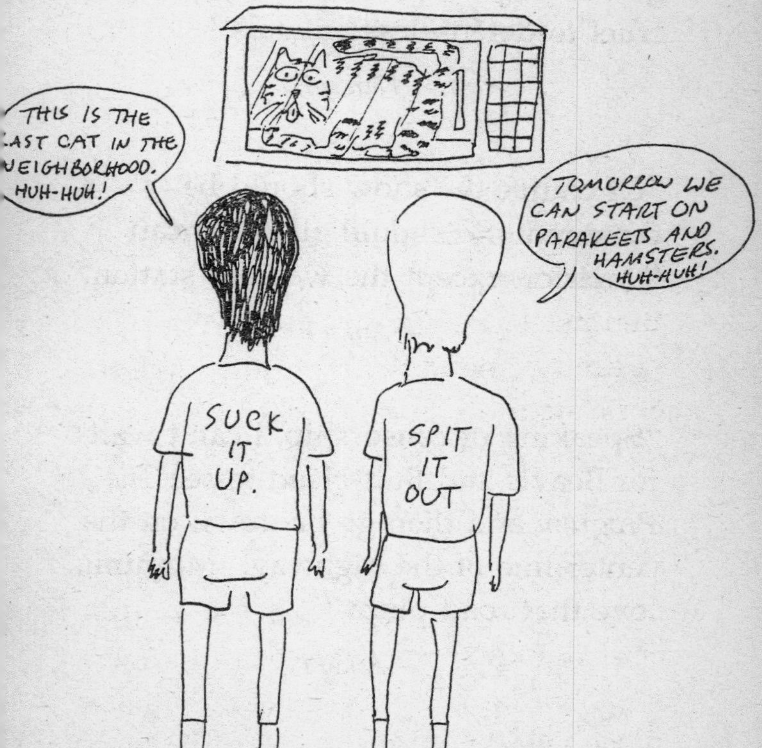
THIS IS THE
LAST CAT IN THE
NEIGHBORHOOD.
HUH-HUH!
TOMORROW WE
CAN START ON
PARAKEETS AND
HAMSTERS.
HUH-HUH!
SUCK
IT
UP.
SPIT
IT
OUT

problem with *Beavis and Butt-Head* is that you've got humans torturing animals. That is not funny cartoon mayhem among animal equals. Kids will identify with these sick cartoon guys and get a power trip by being cruel to defenseless animals."

— *Nancy F.*

"Of course the show should be censured. So should all American television except the weather station."

— *Amin B.*

"Speaking of censorship, I can't wait for Beavis and Butt-Head to see *The Program* and then go lie down on the center line of the highway. Mmmm... love that road pizza."

— *Andy P.*

"MTV had to change the time to avoid young kids from watching destructive things being done with household items like matches. It is different from seeing automatic rifles or chain saws on TV. Five-year-olds can't get their little hands on those things.

— *Pamela L.*

"This moving the time of *Beavis and Butt-Head* was just terrible. By ten-thirty I've got to be out of the T.V. room. And there's no use watching T.V. after ten. By then my homework's done."

— *Fran B.*

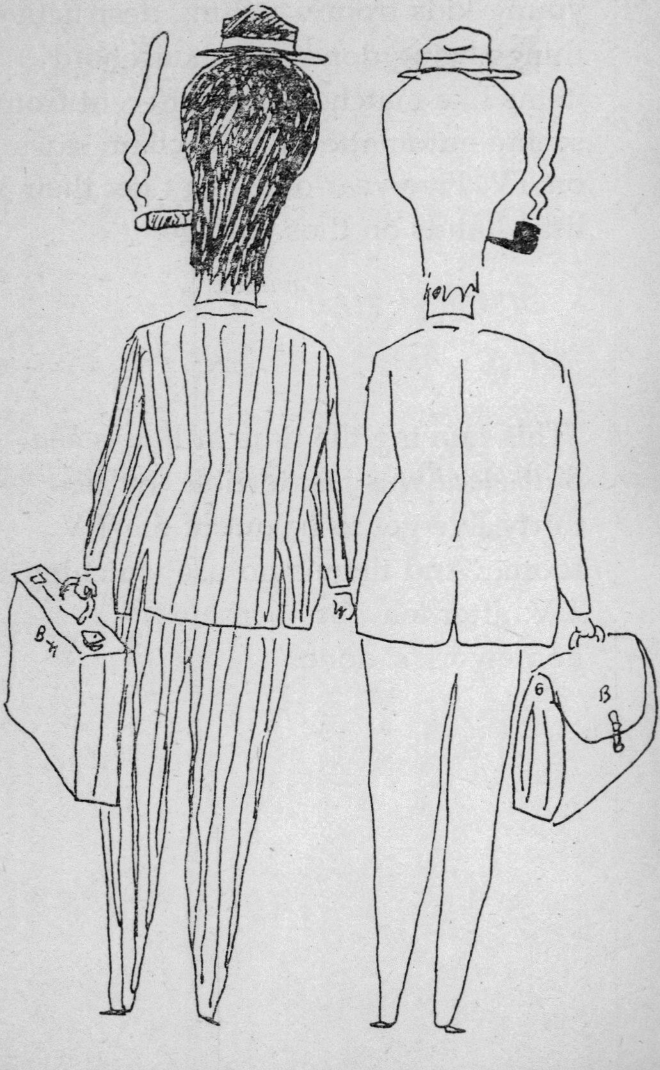

CHAPTER FIVE

Beavis And Butt-Head When They Grow Up

Students sketch a picture of what they see Beavis and Butt-Head doing in the future ... perhaps working at a job as critics, advertising copywriters or salesmen.

STUDENTS SKETCH A PICTURE OF WHAT THEY SEE BEAVIS AND BUTT-HEAD DOING IN THE FUTURE ... PERHAPS WORKING AT A JOB AS CRITICS, ADVERTISING COPYWRITERS OR SALESMEN.

"They should be our ambassadors to Iraq."

– *Ali I.*

"I sense a strong interest in gynecology."

– *Fred Z.*

"They will definitely end up as high school gym teachers. They'll be looking up girls' skirts and sweating like the bungholes in my school."

– *Malissa N.*

"Those morons could never hold down a job. Unless it's something like a Supreme Court Justice."

– *Mark D.*

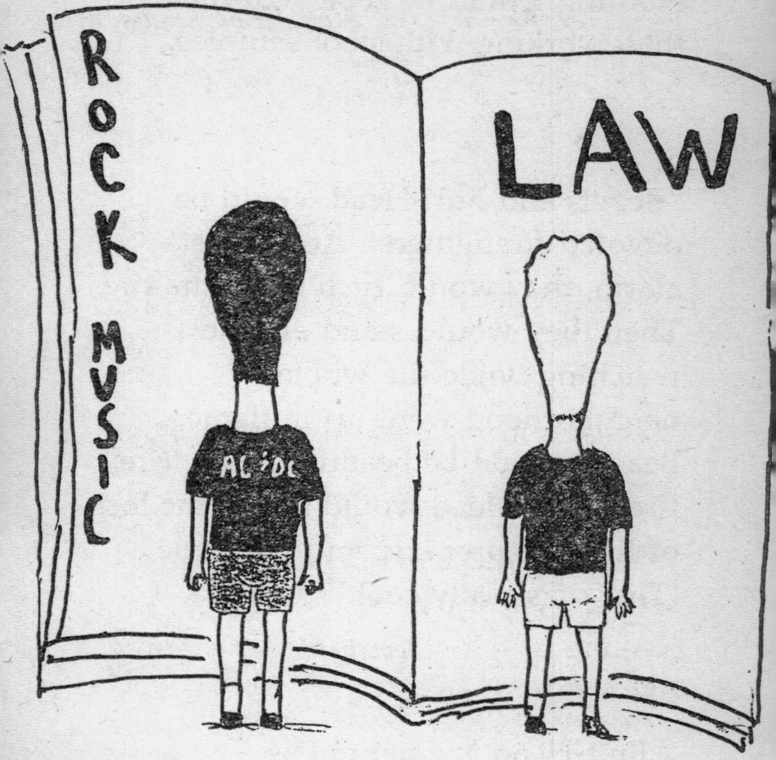
ROCK MUSIC
LAW
AC/DC

"They have a future in medicine. Nothing would be cooler for them than working with stool samples."

— *Sammy T.*

"Beavis and Butt-Head would be devoted firefighters. At the first alarm, they would rush off to the fire. Then they would stand around watching while the whole neighborhood went up in flames. Beavis would be beaming, 'Fire, fire, fire!' Butt-Head would assess the loss of life and property and conclude, 'That was really cool.'

— *Beverly M.*

" Butt-Head is a natural as spokesperson for Charmin bathroom tissues. Can't you hear him tell Mr. Whipple, 'Don't squeeze the buttwipes, huh-huh."

— *Manny F.*

"They might end up as mail carriers in the Antarctic. Cool. Really cool."

— *Janey R.*

"Soon we'll see them on TV selling Butt-Munch breakfast cereal. The official cereal of Jeffrey Dahmer. 'Try Butt-Munch. The crunchy chocolate cereal that you can't just suck'"

— *Freddie G.*

"I wouldn't rule out speech therapy or the clergy."

— *Irvin B.*

"Can't you just hear them do the weather and sports after that butt-wipe Peter Jennings finishes the news. 'Here's Butt-Head's five-day forecast: pretty cool, cool, sucks, sucks, partly sucks. ... And after these words we'll find out from Beavis which teams kicked butt today, and which ones sucked.'"

— *Alvin S.*

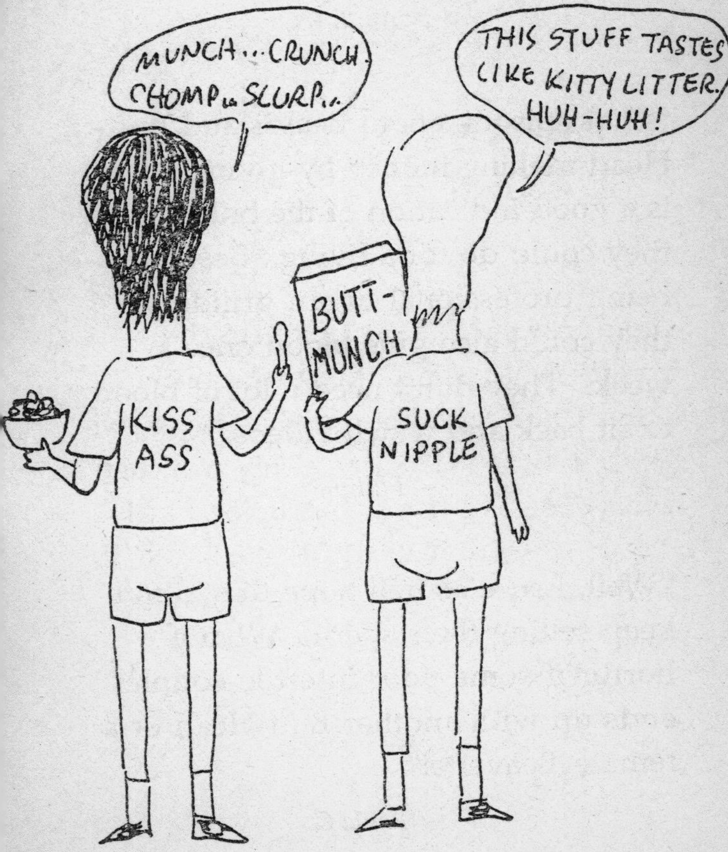
MUNCH... CRUNCH.
CHOMP... SLURP...
THIS STUFF TASTES LIKE KITTY LITTER. HUH-HUH!
BUTT-MUNCH
KISS ASS
SUCK NIPPLE

"Beavis and Butt-Head will be famous one day as the founders of the A.S.P.C.A. — the American Society for the Perpetuation of Cruelty to Animals."

— *Amin B.*

"That episode about Beavis and Butt-Head making money by giving sperm is a good indication of the only thing they could do for a living. Besides being professional organ grinders, they could also give blood once a week. They don't need a lot of blood to sit back and watch videos."

— *Philip P.*

"Well, I sure as hell hope they don't keep selling their sperm. What a horror if some poor infertile couple ends up with another Butt-Head or a female Beavette!"

— *Paula G.*

"There's a name for what Beavis and Butt-Head will be in ten years — bikers."

— *Brad K.*

"They would have to sell something like Dirt Devils, portable vacuum cleaners with six interchangeable butt-heads. This way they can handle dirt bags for a living. Also, they can talk about things that really suck. 'Buy this Port-o-vac — it sucks real cool, heh, heh...'"

— *Ralph L.*

(continued)

B&B Class Humor

Why did Beavis and Butt-Head get kicked out of history class when asked about George Washington and Thomas Jefferson?

> Because they said these were the last two white dudes with those last names.

"They should be video jocks. Maybe by the time they are twenty-five MTV will let a jock say if a video really sucks."

— Ann B.

"I can see Beavis the firefly doing an historic impression of Emperor Nero. Fiddling with himself while Rome burns."

— Cal B.

"Butt-Head will have a distinguished career in television, replacing Allistair Cooke as the aristocratic host of a series of fine dramatic presentations from Great Britain. The name of the show will be "Masterbate Theatre."

— Hadley W.

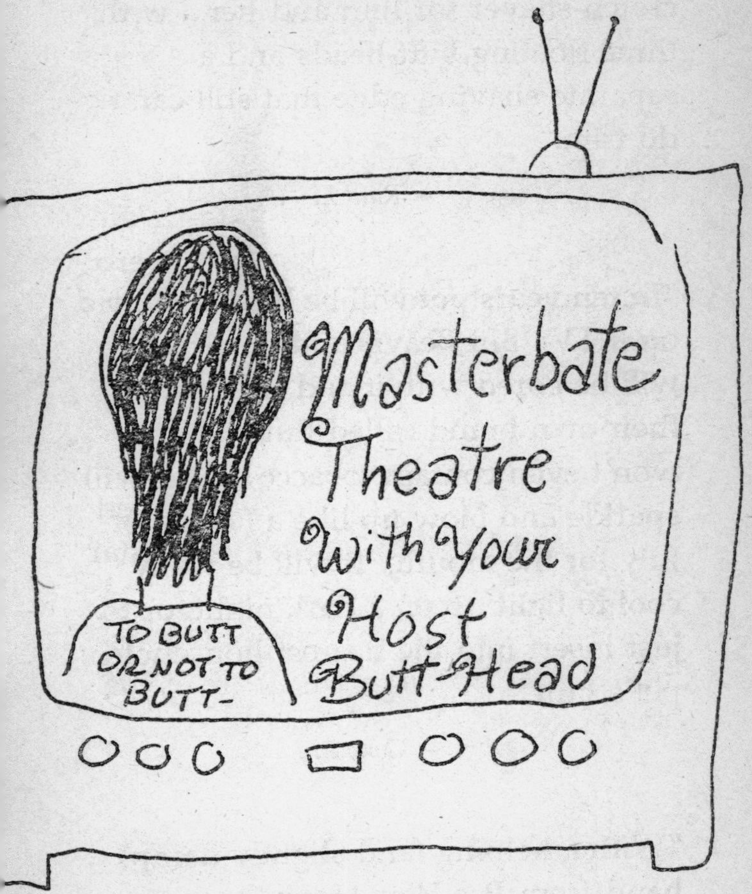
Masterbate
Theatre
With Your
Host
Butt-Head
TO BUTT
OR NOT TO
BUTT-

"The B & B line of consumer goods will feature the Beave 'n Butt electric crotch-shaver for him and her... with three floating butt-heads and a separate shaving edge that still can't do trim."

— *Raul L.*

"In ten years pot will be legal and sold on MTV. But Beavis and Butt-Head will be bored with it and will start their own brand called Butts. Butts won't even contain tobacco, but it will sparkle and blow up like a Fourth of July for the mouth. It will be really cool to light up on a dark night, or to just insert into the nearest household pet's butt."

— *Gene P.*

"With a helping (and slightly damp) hand from Pee Wee Herman, the two boys go on create a new line of

Romance/Self-Help books. Their motto is: 'Forget self-esteem, get steamy by yourself.' Their do-it-yourself mini-books without words ('words suck') are designed to be light enough for wussie bumwipes like themselves to hold up with just the left hand. The porn industry presents them with the Peeyoolitzer Prize, but nobody offers to shake their hand.

— *No Name*

Beavis and Butt-Head: The Next Degeneration...

(continued)

B&B Class Humor
━━━━━━━━━━━━━━━━━━━━━━━━━━━━

Why did Beavis get kicked out of history class?

> 💣 He thought Lincoln was Jewish because he was shot in the temple.

In the year 2530 Beavis and Butt-Head will be brought before a tribunal on the starship Enterprise. It wasn't enough that they accidently recharted the ship's course after saying "yer' anus" in front of the bridge's voice-command computer. Now, they've been caught, red-handed, trying to beam up Ahura's micromini. Captain Kirk points an accusing finger at our heroes and says, "These are the voyeurs of the starship Enterprise..."

— *Lee J.*

"Butt-Head will be pulling in 200 grand as the new Ed MacMahon who sits there and laughs — heh-heh — at every stupid joke made by the talk show host. And then we'll see his face on 200 million pieces of junk mail telling us how we may have already won five million dollars."

— *Larry L.*

BEHIND BEAVIS AND BUTT-HEAD • 107

It takes a tough turkey to hire tender turdwipes like Beavis and Butt-Head, but their first real job comes from America's billionaire chicken king with the bald head and funny ears — that's right, Ross Perot. At first Beavis was assigned to the chicken parts factory, but he kept saying things like, "Huh-huh, you said breasts." So soon he was sent alongside Butt-Head to the giant incubator where they swept away egg fragments and got to tell friends about all the naked chicks they saw.

— *Samantha L.*

I have a real Butt-Head for Health right now, so I can see Butt-Head from MTV lecturing us on date rape:
"Uhm... hello class, today I am supposed to speak to you about, huh-huh, date rape. Let's see... it says here, 'Date rape is no laughing

matter' — huh-huh, huh-huh. 'It could happen to anyone.'

I wish it could happen to me, huh-huh. Uhm... 'You should set time limits for your date.' That's right, I'm supposed to talk about a few curs, or was that cur-fews? Uhm... you should never be late to your date rape. I know I always come too early. Oh, wait... premature jackalation is another topic. What was I talking about? Oh yes, date rape. Uhm ... it says here, 'Date rape can occur in seemingly safe conditions, when other people are around.' That's right, class. If you have a good friend, like my Beaver — I mean Beavis, then you can even go somewhere for a double

(continued)

B&B Class Humor

Why did Butt-Head get kicked out of health class?

> 💣* Because he thought hormones were noises that hookers made.

date rape. Anyway, there's more to read in this chapter ... but words suck. If you have any really cool date rape experiences... please share. Even better, if you've got any home videos..."

— Al R.

Beavis and Butt-Head are bound to be hired as scabs in the next strike of air-traffic controllers. First they'll ask for the scabs to pick on, then they'll be taught how to guide incoming pilots to the airport runways. That bug-zapping light will go off in their head, and they will get two 747's to meet on the same runway for spectacular results:

"Air India, you're clear for jerk-off, huh-huh, on runway 7-11.

"Pakistan Air, you're clear for landing at 7-11. And get me some beef jerky and a big slurpy, huh-huh."

BEHIND BEAVIS AND BUTT-HEAD • 111

CRASH!

"Huh-huh. That was real cool, Beavis."

"Yah, Butt-Head, fire, fire, fire!"

"Hey, Beavis, now tune your headphone to the rock station. It looks like a real butt-kicking video out there on the runway, with all the flashing red lights and fire hoses."

"That's right, Butt-Head. We gotta make a video of this. Then we'll get back on MTV."

— *Michael F.*

"Beavis would want to sell a product he can light up. He'll probably sell Kool cigarettes. The big tag line: 'They're Kool, and they don't suck.'"

— *Mason D.*

CHAPTER SIX
The Best Beavis And Butt-Head Jokes

MANY BEAVIS AND BUTT-HEAD JOKES ARE CIRCULATING AROUND THE SCHOOLS. WHAT ARE YOUR FAVORITES?

MANY BEAVIS AND BUTT-HEAD JOKES ARE CIRCULATING AROUND THE SCHOOLS. WHAT ARE YOUR FAVORITES?

Here are some of the favorites collected and edited by Allen Nelson....

Beavis and Butt-Head's Family

Why do Beavis and Butt-Head's parents keep monkeys as pets?

> 💣 **For replacement parts**

What did Beavis and Butt-Head's moms give them to play with in the pool?

> 💣 **Toasters.**

How did Beavis and Butt-Head's moms stop them from bedwetting?

> 💣 **They got them electric blankets.**

How was Butt-Head annoying everyone at his dad's high school reunion?

> 💣 He kept trying to look up his dad's old girlfriends.

Who are America's most eloquent spokespersons for abortion?

> 💣 Beavis and Butt-Heads' parents.

Out-takes from Beavis and Butt-Head's Historic Meeting With President Clinton

With what song did Beavis and Butt-Head welcome President Clinton?

💣 **In-hale to the Chief.**

What's as exciting as Al Gore giving a speech?

💣 **Beavis and Butt-Head evaluating music videos.**

Why did Beavis think the 1992 election was too violent for MTV to show?

💣 **There was too much Gore!**

What Clinton Administration job did the president offer Butt-Head?

> 💣 **Secretery of the Posterior.**

How did Beavis advise President Clinton to deal with the Gennifer Flowers problem?

> 💣 **He suggested that he let Ted Kennedy drive her home.**

How did Attorney General Janet Reno explain the Waco, Texas tragedy and the Malibu firestorms?

> 💣 **She blamed it on Beavis and Butt-Head wannabees who watched MTV.**

How did Butt-Head explain Roger Clinton's behavior?

> He was a cross between Billy Carter and Ted Kennedy.

How does Beavis explain the marriage of a Kennedy girl to Arnold Shwarzenegger?

> Somebody's trying to breed a bulletproof Kennedy.

BEAVIS AND BUTT-HEAD AT LARGE

Why do Beavis and Butt-Head tape their report cards to their cars' license plates?

💣 **So they can legally park in handicapped zones.**

How did Beavis and Butt-Head find out about Pee Wee Herman's crime?

💣 **They had first-hand knowledge.**

Why is Butt-Head like a nature photographer?

💣 **They both like to blow up little animals.**

ROAD
KILL
POSSUM
GUTS

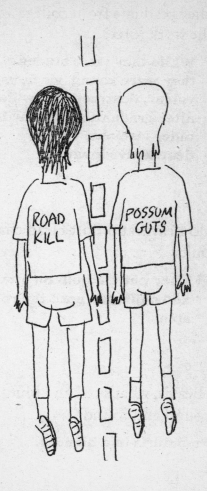

How will Beavis and Butt-Head change when they graduate from college and enter the work force?

> 💣 While they were students, they were young, viscious, vulgar, destructive lowlifes; after graduating, they will be older viscious, vulgar destructive lowlifes.

How do Beavis and Butt-Head change a light bulb?

> 💣 They put the bulb on a table and sniff glue until the room spins.

"Hey Beavis, what's red and blue, and goes round and round?"

> 💣 Smurfs in a blender.

What's the difference between Beavis and Butt-Head and dogs?

> 💣 **Most dogs have better hair cuts.**

Why didn't Beavis and Butt-Head go to their local cat show?

> 💣 **They ran out of firecrackers.**

How did Beavis think Captain Hook died?

> 💣 **By wiping himself with the wrong hand.**

Why did the *Beavis and Butt-Head* show recieve an award from the American Medical Association?

> 💣 **Because they made so many parents and cat lovers sick.**

What did Beavis call a black kid who called him Butt-Head?

💣 **Butt-Wheat.**

Why are Beavis and Butt-Head like something you'd find under your bed?

💣 **They're a dirty pair of loafers.**

Why are Beavis and Butt-Head just like broken rifles?

💣 **They won't work and it's hard to fire them.**

What's black and brown and would look great on Beavis and Butt-Head?

💣 **Two Dobermans.**

What did the police say when they strapped Beavis and Butt-Head to the electric chair?

> 💣 **More power to you, butt-wipes!**

What did Beavis and Butt-Head do when they heard about the starving people in Somalia and Bosnia?

> 💣 **They were so bummed that they went on a CD buying spree.**

"Hey Beavis, which hand do you use to wipe your butt with?"
"Uhm, my right hand."
"That's gross! At least I use butt-wipes.

Why did Beavis and Butt-Head decide they would not go on an around-the-world trip?

> 💣 **Because they had no way of getting back.**

What's the most effective way to shut up Beavis and Butt-Head?

> 💣 **Ask them what they really think.**

How dos the dictionary define "juvenile delinquent?"

> 💣 **With a picture of Beavis and Butt-Head.**

What is the definition of "redundant?"

> 💣 **Telling Beavis and Butt-Head to forget it.**

What's scarier than Dan Quayle as president of the U.S.?

> 💣 **Beavis and Butt-Head showing up at your home with the moving company.**

Why was Butt-Head jealous of Jeffrey Dahmer?

> 💣 **He just reachd into the fridge to get a piece of ass.**

How would Beavis turn down Jeffrey Dahmer's advances?

> 💣 **He'd say, "Over my dead body!"**

Why couldn't Beavis and Butt-Head get circumcised?

> 💣 **Because there's no end to those two crazy weinerheads.**

Why did Mickey Mouse throw Beavis and Butt-Head out of Disney World?

💣* **They were trying to sell Bill Clinton watches!**

What is Beavis' favorite martial art?

💣* **Kick buttsing.**

What do Beavis and Butt-Head have in common with that French Canadian team, the Montreal Expos?

💣* **They both play frog baseball.**

Beavis and Butt-Head on Sexuality

How do Beavis and Butt-Head think the Los Angeles Laker Cheerleaders got AIDS?

> 💣 **By MAGIC!**

What do Beavis and Butt-Head think Ervin Johnson's nickname, MAGIC, stands for?

> 💣 **"My Ass Got Infected, Coach!"**

How did Beavis reject the Judge's offer of a lawyer during his trial for public lewdness?

> 💣 **He said, "I don't need a lawyer, your Honor, I can get myself off."**

What do Beavis and Butt-Head think is Michael Jackson's favorite song?

> 💣 **"Baby Love!"**

What did Beavis and Butt-Head tell their friends when asked if they smoke after having sex?

> 💣 **"We don't know. We never looked! Heh, heh, heh, heh!"**

How do Beavis and Butt-Head define an orgy?

> 💣 **The two of them getting intimate with Rosy Palm and her five sisters.**

How do Beavis and Butt-Head define foreplay?

> 💣 **Pressing all the knobs until they find MTV.**

What do Beavis and Butt-Head call buttus interuptus?

> 💣 When a commercial comes on while their mooning a Madonna video.

Why did Butt-Head beg for a job as a department store Santa?

> 💣 It's the only way any girl would sit on his lap and tell him what she wants.

Why was Beavis kicked out of Sunday school?

> 💣 Because he kept asking where this garden was with the naked people."

CHAPTER SEVEN

The Media's Reaction To Beavis and Butt-Head

Here is an analysis and a synopsis of the most interesting B&B comments that have been inundating the media.

Here is an analysis and a synopsis of the most interesting Beavis and Butt-Head comments that have been inundating the media.

This chapter was prepared by my assistant on this project, Bruce Hodge.

THE EVOLUTION OF A MEDIA PHENOMENON

(OR HOW TWO DORKY TOONS CAME TO RULE THE NATION'S YOUTH, MTV AND THE MUSIC INDUSTRY.)

Written and researched by Bruce Hodge

Beavis and Butt-Head were unleashed on an unsuspecting world in 1989's short cartoon, *Quiet Please*, by creator Mike Judge. The deadbeat duo made a second appearance in 1992's short cartoon *Sittin' Pretty* — in which they attended a monster truck trashathon out in the boonies and rapturously applauded the shredding by combine harvester of an enviromental folk-singer. *The Seattle Times* described them, on November 2, 1992, as "two teenage reactionaries."

If only it had been that simple, or that innocent!

Judge, the aforementioned creator of these abominations in the face of God, Walt Disney and all that is decent — told *Daily Variety* that the idea for the two schnooks' first-ever appearance, a little classic called *Frog Baseball*, came to him from an overheard conversation in which some guy said to his buddy, "Have you ever played a game of frog baseball?" Judge admits that the two people he overheard were, in fact, probably very normal, certifiably sane, even credit worthy individuals, but that he himself, when faced with this simple and innocent phrase, leapt to the mental picture of a Wadsworth '59 3-lb-stainless-steel bat hitting an itty bitty bull-frog out the stadium. Mr. Judge was inspired and made the cartoon.

Judge, who had been an engineer doing cartoons in his spare time and selling them on a freelance basis to the cable networks, drew the two budding sadists who could hit pop-ups with small amphibians ... and lo and behold the daring duo was born. "It's sick," he admitted, "but Beavis and Butt-Head ... these guys are not to be admired."

But it's too late for that, Buddy!

Judge's creation of these little darlings coincided with a desire on MTV's part to expand their programming from simple music videos with intermittent commentator chatter to more elaborate and ambitious cultural analysis, fashion tips, and/or how-to advice from the rich and famous. Needless to say, Beavis and Butt-

Head were perfect for the job. As *Daily Variety* reported, "Some call them the Wayne and Garth from hell." Begging to differ, MTV's creative director and executive VP Judy McGrath said that, to MTV, they were "attitudinally correct."

Initially tried out on MTV's cartoon showcase, "Liquid Television", the duo struck a massive (and probably jarring) chord with their target audience of stay-at-home, throw-the-cat-in-the-tumble-dryer, hang-at-the-mall-and-buy-a-CD youth. MTV had from, its very inception, used many a cartoon to break up the tedium between endless shots of barely musical, barely clothed, barely watchable nubile rockers and their lip-synching model squeezes.

Beavis and Butt-Head were a way of remaking the video jocks of future without any real need for a break with the past. They were young, they were hip and exciting, they rocked. You didn't need to pay them monthly royalties on re-screens and you didn't have to send flowers to their trailer to match their bucket of caviar. They were hired. *Beavis and Butt-Head*, a brand spanking new show, went on the air March 8, 1992.

Playboy was not impressed. They noted that the latest additions to MTV presenter Paulie Shore's "motley crew" of barely literate veejays were "cartoons, literally." And went on to say "Beavis and Butt-Head: two cretins." Surprisingly enough, considering the number of people who buy and, uh, read Playboy for its penetrating cultural analysis, the duo were a riotous success. So much so that by early June *The Buffalo News* could report with some credibility the exaggerated but by no means unfounded story that "no fewer than seven movie deals (and a record deal)" were in the works for the cartoon crack-ups.

It's not that the media were quick to catch on to the concept. The last mentioned paper said of them in the same story that they were "so wondrously young and stupid that Wayne and Garth look like MacNeil and Lehrer by comparison." *The Atlanta Journal and Constituion*, obviously never having seen the show but nevertheless writing about it, called them some sort of *Bill and Ted's Animated Adventure*, thereby missing the true essence, and the subtle brilliance deep in the bowels of Beavis and Butt-Headian humor.

They're not just a couple of celluloid strip felons going "huh-huh-huh" for God's sake! But we'll come back to the deeper meanings later.

One thing nobody has mentioned yet is that

these two little guys were there to sell records and to sell advertising time. Sure, the attention span of most teenagers is limited, but, hey, they don't have mortgages to pay and their money is easy come and very easy go. Beavis and Butt-Head's popularity sells advertising rates for MTV. We don't realize, we tend to forget every little while, that MTV is an all advertising channel since music videos are three-minute commercials for albums.

As MTV's creative director Judy McGrath put it, "We create programming our viewers want to see. This is an audience whose appetite for change is great and whose attention span flags pretty quick." (Uh, that's "quick-*ly*" Judy.) Speaking of the audience of kids, Ms. McGrath went on, "If they don't like it, the advertising won't support it." And she told this to *Billboard*, the advertising man's bible, so you know it must be true.

And Beavis and Butt-Head were remarkably successful at selling space and selling records. Largely because of the very things the generation older than the one watching the cartoon objected to. These sentiments from the *St. Petersburg Times* are representative: "Between innings of *Frog Baseball*, where they swat a helpless amphibian into oblivion...quite frankly, Beavis and Butt-Head are idiots."

The article went on to complain of Beavis's pimpled rear-end mooning a bad video, the pair sniffing gas over the open stove top to get a buzz (seeing sloppy little cartoon stars spinning around over their heads), and setting fire to a cat, just for the cruel joy of it. Needless to say, the grownups were not amused.

Congress was ready to propose TV censorship. A pre-emptive strike by the networks was desperately needed. On June 30, 1993, TV network executives staged a gala to announce plans to attach warning labels to violent TV shows. Now, it must be noted that Beavis and Butt-Head, bless their little celluloid-painted hearts, already had warnings included in the program. For example, in one sequence, the stove-gas sniffing incident already mentioned, the little sloppy stars circling their heads were accompanied by a caption popping up on the screen:

"If you are not a cartoon, stove gas WILL KILL YOU."

Then the dynamic duo light a match and the house explodes. But maybe that's not what the TV executives and, more to the point, the

House of Representatives, had in mind.

You see, the networks didn't dream up this warnings concept out of marketing concerns, which is all they ever dream about. According to Tony Snow of *The Detroit News*, Senator Howard Metzenbaum, (Ohio), warned TV executives in May, 1993 that "If you just do nothing... we're going to come down on you harder than you would like us to." Representative John Bryant of Texas joined the chorus with, "These guys are not going to do anything unless we hold a club over their heads." In other words, the TV executives had some incentives here.

The heads of ABC, CBS, NBC, Fox and the Motion Picture Association of America, never ones to force a confrontation if they can weazle out of it, locked their collective lawyers in a room. Some six weeks later the lawyers emerged with this formula: "Due to some violent content, parental caution advised."

Since the disclaimer did not affect cable stations, which serve sixty percent of today's viewing audience, and since it was agreed that it would appear for only two years thereafter and since such warnings only serve to whet the appetite of teenagers, pre-teens and children — all this amounted to zip.

The learned gentlemen of Congress, of course, disagreed: "This is the dawning of a new era," declared Rep. Cogressman Edward Markey (Massachussetts). Markey's committee having been engaged in harassing networks for the last sixteen years, it seems marginally in his interest to declare this outcome a blockbuster. More relevantly, he added: "For the last 40 years the debate has been whether violence on television affects antisocial behavior. Today we can put an end to that debate."

In other words, for forty years TV executives maintained the argument that you cannot prove any damage was done to viewers, so you cannot justify any legal restraints. With this act of submission some are claiming they threw that whole moral position away. "Moral position" may seem a strong way of putting it, but a precedent was set by the TV executives' caving in. As Tony Snow's article points out, "Self-described television watchdog groups have made it clear that they consider labels a first step toward a more comprehensive system of government control." Having gotten the TV executives to cede the moral argument that no connection can be proved between violence (and other social ills) and broadcasted material, the would be censors in our midst now have a clear line of argument to pick on any target they choose.

Which is not to say that we here investigating the phenomenon of these two lovable cartoon cut-ups have strong views on the television/violence argument. We do, however, have strong views about Congressmen and their motives for trying to legislate TV viewing. The real approaches to solving these problems do not make the best of sound-bites for a politician to try and sell over the air, nor do they lend themselves to quick and easy legislation on the part of Congress. In a phrase: stopping violence doesn't get votes. It's too hard and too complicated and it's not easy for anyone to see you doing it. LOOKING like you're doing something about violence is much easier, AND it makes for GREAT TV come election time.

SO, instead of trying to solve a problem, you look for a way to get lots of publicity as you TALK about solving it. And where is the best place to get publicity? On TV.

Those of us who fear media censorship don't have to look hard to find an instructive historical parallel. The previous venture of Congress into showbiz legislation, with the House Un-American Activities Committee, was led by the infamous junior senator from West Virginia named Joseph McCarthy. The real reasons THEY wanted to investigate the content of entertainment back then? They SAID it was to protect America from Communism. The historical record shows that instead they turned the hearings into an effective force for intimidation and repression of ideas.

The infamous McCarthy hearings served no real national security purpose for the same reason that the warning label on TV programs serves no real purpose: These congressional panels are not always geared to solving a problem but rather to gaining publicity for their members. Arthur Miller, one of the most famous writers to be called before the House Un-American Activities Committee, recalls in his memoirs, *Timebends,* that one Congressman on the committee offered to excuse him from testifying and any possible legal proceedings if he would only arrange a photo-op for the committee with Miller's then-wife Marylin Monroe.

Oh, yes, the wheels of justice are swift, and in the Halls of Congress they are always turning!

Back to Beavis and Butt-Head and TV legislation — Tony Snow further argued that Cain did not slay Abel because of "a vivid docudrama" and that "people who commit violent acts are bad people, not saints who went bad after watching re-runs of *Charlie's Angels*." Whether you agree with that or not, it does seem questionable that people who cannot balance their own collective checkbook should presume to decide what we spend our own time and money watching.

On July 8th, 1993, news programs reported that a reward of $11,000 was being offered by cat owner Barbara Hijduk, for information leading to the arrest of the person or persons who blew up her cat with firecrackers. Animal rights activists, among them Lisa Juday of the Santa Cruz SPCA, linked this act to TV programs showing acts of violence against animals and named *Beavis and Butt-Head* in particular. An episode alluding to a feline firecracker adventure had aired five days before. MTV released a statement that "the MTV audience is aware that [Beavis and Butt-Head] are cartoon characters not to be imitated," but conceded that animals had been used as playthings on the show.

One immediate reaction to the exploding cat story came from Marin County California, where lottery winning millionaire and former TV producer Dick Zimmerman saw the story on the news and decided to take action against the offending toons. Having won $7.1 million dollars in the California state lottery, Zimmerman was also in a position to do something about it. He set up a "Beavis and Butt-Head" line for callers to share their outrage over the latest cartoon or to join the crusade to have the diminutive duo removed. The number was (415)-485-2687, as reported by the *Hollywood Reporter*, and calls flooded in from parents, schoolteachers, nannies, and all others offended by our pimply-faced chums.

Carol Robinson, MTV's senior vice president in charge of press relations, responded that Zimmerman seemed misinformed as to the contents of the show and that there had been no single episode during which Beavis and Butt-Head did that particular thing to a cat. The kitty-cide was "a horrible thing, but it's a real reach to blame it on Beavis and Butt-Head."

Others thought differently, but those outside of Congress had good reason to moderate their publicly stated views. For one thing, Beavis and Butt-Head were selling records. In the words of one Mercury label executive: "The White Zombies sold 7,000 units last week on a year-old album that got little response the first time out." This was on the basis of a favorable review from two people who didn't really exist. He went on to say: "Beavis and Butt-Head are legitimately selling records."

Other executives noticed a distinct "sales spike" in the figures of an album every time the show featuring a positive review from our toon friends was run.

MTV's senior vice president of music and talent pointed out the great immunity that Beavis and Butt-Head enjoyed as reviewers. On the one hand, most people realized that "any attention is a good thing" and took the show for what it was: "two metalhead kids who don't like dance videos or wimpy ballads." On the other hand if bands or executives did take offence at what the inky twins said about them they had a real problem: "You'd feel pretty stupid complaining about it. What would you say? These two cartoons are picking on me?"

This left MTV with a very hot and lucrative property, as metal bands vied to get their videos reviewed on the show. Most bands were hoping they would be spared the mini-maulers caustic comment, but they unable to do much about it if their video got trashed with remarks like, "Beavis, change the channel or kill me or this sucks!" And all the while MTV was swamped with calls from all the bands asking for any and every bit of Beavis and Butt-Head merchandise available.

MTV covered itself by starting each show with a "disclaimer" stating that "Beavis and Butt-Head are not real. They are stupid cartoon people — dumb, crude, thoughtless, ugly, sexist, self-destructive fools. But for some reason the little wiener-heads make us laugh." As noted above, such disclaimers seldom have effect. This one can even be said to act as a sort of ironic advertisement of the twosome's most appealing features to their target audience.

And yet MTV let itself be seen as doing its duty. The episode that had our heroes sniffing paint thinner included the humorous disclaimer, "Breathing pain thinner will damage your brain. Look what it's done to Beavis and Butt-Head."

There was one episode in which a cat was painted. No doubt, like the frog baseball masterpiece, animals were being used "as playthings." No mention has been made of a disclaimer on that show, if there was any. Perhaps, since that adventure did not constitute a risk to *human* life, it was not percieved as being necesary. But the real reason for the light-heartedness of the disclaimers was different.

Carol Robinson summed up the toon terrors' legal and social standing in this way: "You can't put them in the same category as real people. They are animated characters and can get away with things that people can't."

Then a little boy burnt down his mother's trailer and killed his two year old sister.

But before we get to the burning trailer, we need a few more words on why exactly these two terrors are so popular. *Newsday* ran a story on them on July 25, 1993 in which they noted that Beavis and Butt-Head had become MTV's most popular half-hour show, that they were the latest in a long line of dolts to fascinate the American public. The lineage includes *The Three Stooges*, Archie Bunker the lovable racist and sexist, airheads Wayne and Garth of "Wayne's World", and fellow toons *The Simpsons*. This lineage of dolts finally ends with the lowest possible common denominator imaginable — our beloved all-American boys from MTV.

In a phrase that reads rather differently in the light of recent events concerning a burnt trailer, Beavis is characterized as having "a blond pompadour" and being "probably a clinical pyromaniac."

Several different theories of their appeal then emerged. One was that they were basically boys, fourteen-year-old, socially dysfunctioal boys: "obssessed with bodily functions, the female body, the inherent coolness of heavy metal music and committing .. mayhem." Key witnesses in favor of this theory are such people as Christina Kelly, editor of *Sassy* magazine: "Everybody has a little bit of Beavis and Butt-Head in them. It's boy humor."

She notes that some of it goes "over her head," but that when she watches it with boys they are in stitches. She adds that while they are "moronic", some of the stuff they say "is really right on. The videos they tear apart really stink."

And this is the reason, according to second witness Kurt Andersson, media essayist of *Time* magazine, that they appeal to kids— they are accurate in their judgements as to what's bull and what isn't, and they are accurate in their reflection of the lives of their young viewers:

"It's TV literally reflecting their lives rather than some fakey, sitcom reconstruct.... It's a fresh depiction of how a lot of American youth really live and are."

Or, as creator Mike Judge puts it: "Maybe they're popular because they're characters that are sort of everywhere, you just don't see them on TV that often."

The growing legions of over-twenty and over-thirty viwers are accounted for by the, for want of a better word, "culture" argument, in its various forms.

Newsday calls them "a moronic, minimalist Siskel and Ebert" talking over the videos. While the oldsters may be put off by the crude humor, they are taken just as much as the youngsters by the accuracy of the sarcasm and wide-range of pop-culture references. There is a savyness about TV and its business to the show as the twosome watch MTV at the same time as their viewers do, thus generating cameraderie between the cartoons and the home audience which often turns into a participation event as real viewers agree with the rambunctious cartoons' analysis of MTV videos. The result is a unique "TV fun-house mirror" effect that "drives" other cutting-edge shows like *Late Night With David Letterman* and *The Larry Sanders Show*. Both of these shows appeal to intelligent as well as populist audiences by often commenting on the crassness of the medium itself.

Finally, maybe the crudity doesn't put off as many hip grown-ups as you might think. In the words of the show's executive producer Abby Terkuhle: "They are so politically incorrect in a politically correct time that [they are] a breath of fresh air."

Or, as Judge puts it, "It's a kind of therapy to see something completely stupid and pointless. Who knows?"

It must be noted that Judge seems not to be one of the legions that find the show to be simple fun. When he created the pair he was "going on pure instinct" and, as he says, "probably against my better judgement." For a while there he was embarrassed to show the cartoon to anyone. Most notably to show it to his wife of five years who, apparently, is "still getting used" to the show's particular brand of whoopee.

At ease or not, the cartoon comrades' popularity soon found Judge at the head of a team of twenty animators and six writers, producing the twenty-eight cartoons or so needed to begin a full season on MTV. And later would come the endless merchandising: tee-shirts, halloween masks (the duo were the most popular mask this Halloween across the country), baseball caps, posters, lunch-boxes, books and movies. What else could these tiny titans sell?

But, maybe an element of Judge's embarrassment was justified. Back with the important question of what these two cartoons mean and do to children.

On the one hand, there seems to be little disagreement that Beavis and Butt-Head are stupid. Mark Lehman, 25, editor of *Dirt*, a "hip magazine for 14 to 22 year old males", says, "These people are like cockroaches — and I mean that in the nicest possible way." They will never evolve.

But is that truly representative of how teenagers and younger kids feel?

In *The Times-Picayune* of July 25, columnist Angus Lind, found a different spin on the question of the show's popularity with teens and younger children when he questioned a sixteen-year-old as to the show's appeal. "They think they're the best —even though the show makes 'em out to be the biggest losers and some of the ugliest people you've ever seen in your life."

In other words, much like many of their viewers, the two have unsatisfactory lives in many ways, but assume an attitude and bravado that their viewers admire, however stupid and self-destructive it might prove in real life. But the crucial passage in their analysis is what follows:

"They're people other people wish they

could be but don't dare to — like being foul-mouthed to elders or teachers, or any authority."

Or burning a trailer with an authority figure in it, may one ask?

On July 31st, 1993, Dick Zimmerman, now claiming to have received hundreds of calls on open line for the crusade against Beavis and Butt-Head, told *Billboard* that he did not "blame the media for society's problems" and that he understood "the evil of talking about or suggesting censorship in a free society". His only goal was "to open rational conversation between the citizens of this country and the media that serve those citizens."

August's *Rolling Stone* cover splashed Beavis and Butt-Head onto news stands across the nation. Inside, writer Charles Young suggested that the teen terrors were no more harmful than Bugs Bunny, that some of us once were not unlike Beavis and Butt-Head, and that, this being a satire, if they were nice kids they would — by definition — not be funny.

Terry Rakolta, President of Americans For Responsible Television, told the media that MTV was responsible for showing this program to a too-young audience at a too-early time slot (seven PM, one at eleven PM, Monday to Thursday.) Rakolta claimed that the cartoon characters were showing children how to sniff paint thinner and play with lighters.

The *Daily Telegraph* of England, in the column of its U.S. correspondent Tony Parsons, noted that Beavis and Butt-Head were "being called the voice of a new generation." Also that Beavis's remarks about videos took such forms as: "Not enough fire...I like fire. Fire! Fire!" Also that the show's disclaimers both superimposed and within the text of the show were not necessarily effective. "I like to burn stuff," Butt-Head said in one episode, "But that doesn't mean that you have to." He paused, then snickered. "Huh-huh! Huh-huh! Huh-huh! It would be cool if you did though."

On August 29th the prestigious *New York Times* called the summer of 1993 "the summer of...Beavis and Butt-Head."

That same day a column by Tom Maurstad in the *Dallas Morning News* made some very astute points. Firstly, that the twosome were "unfailingly truthful" in their responses. (Whether they were too stupid to lie was another question). Secondly, that they are not really video critics, but portraits of the ninety percent of the audience watching videos who, in creator Mike Judge's words, see some arty and symbolic video full of high artistic ambition and are "just going huh-huh, huh-huh, what's this?"

It is this quality which led various media figures to read the two, with their condemnation of MTV itself and its general failure to play the very videos Beavis and Butt-Head like anywhere else but during their show, as "an indictment" not just of MTV, but the "godless, illiterate, media-saturated, crumbling-infrastructure, disintegrating-family times that have spawned MTV." They are, literally, emblems of everything that's wrong with kids today — in the view of adults.

They are the "archetypal products of the MTV generation." Hence *Rolling Stone* called them the voice of that generation.

Beavis and Butt-Head are the next step down the evolutionary or historical ladder from the so-called Generation X of post-yuppies who, legend has it, quit their stellar career jobs to hop on a motorbike and see the real China. Beavis and Butt-Head are lower down the evolutionary ladder than even Wayne and Garth! Wayne has his own cable-access show; he managed to go downtown, fill some forms, take a video production course, etc. Beavis and Butt-Head, however, can barely make it to school once a day. Indeed, Mike Judge notes that "part of their charm is that they're not too ambitious and not very functional."

Nor is it a historical coincidence that the "demographic" that has been branded by the media as "an underemployed generation of drifting slackers who can look forward to a significantly lower standard of living than their parents" should be buying up every cup, shirt, hat and poster they can get their hands on with the beloved cartoon images on it. These are heroes who, as Butt-Head told *Rolling Stone*, believe:

"If you go to school and like, study and stuff? And grow up and get a job at a company, and, like, get promoted? You have to go there and do stuff that sucks for the rest of your life."

Much like the insight cited by the sixteen—year old, that these guys were losers but they "think they're the best"—Beavis and Butt-Head make a first-strike rejection of the job market which will reject them. The future no longer holds any options to fulfill young people's dreams. Neither Generation X nor Beavis and Butt-Head's generation are giving up the money their predecessors in the 1980s made. It just isn't there anymore, so they adjust their stated goals and don't chase it.

Getting back to the dynamic dimwits, on September 4, 1993, *Billboard* carried a story by Deborah Russell charting the ever larger sales figures a plug or even a trashing by Beavis and Butt-Head on MTV could mean for an album. The band White Zombie was still pushing up The Billboard 200 eighteen months after its album "La Sexcorcisto: Devil Music Vol.1" had initially been released. A thumbs-up from the diminutive daddyos for the group Corrosion of Conformity's clip "Dance of the Dead" pushed their average album sales up to 800 units a week for four weeks running. As their director of video promotion, Mark Klein, put it, even if they got slammed by the teeny tikes "any exposure is better than no exposure."

This was not an uncommon sentiment. Once the link between Butt-Head and big sales was established, MTV's phone didn't stop ringing with calls from promotion people clawing and grabbing for spots on the playlist. Rick Krim, MTV Vice President of talent and artist relations noted, "People seemed willing to get on the show even if the clip got trashed."

Beavis, you're a star! When they're lining up to get slammed by you, you got 'em where you want 'em. Uh-huh, uh-huh, uh-huh, uh-huh!

Novelist T. Jefferson Parker summed up many people's perception of the teeny terrorists' attitude in a column in *The Los Angeles Times* where he imagined a letter sent to an agony column by someone from the Beavis and Butt-Head generation:

"Dear Cool Dude: My mother is a hopeless invalid and has been bedridden for months. I finally sold enough of her disability checks to buy a new wardrobe. So what should I get?"

Grown-up disapproval sells. Pocket Books paid a reported $800,000 for "Beavis and Butt-Head: This Book Sucks," a book about our heroes.

On September 20th, 1993, Secretary of Education Richard Riley mentioned our heroes in an address to the *Fortune Magazine* Education Summit Conference in Washington, an audience of business and education luminaries. His closing remarks were about "the friendly monster television" and its impact on education.

"Children love *Barney*, and that's great. *Beavis and Butt-Head* are here to stay. I'm sure of that."

Then he noted a correlation proved between the number of hours children watched television and the decline of reading skills, in direct proportion to whether they watched three hours of TV a day, or four to six or more. In conclusion, he sounded a note which would recur within the month from another quarter of the government but with harsher emphasis:

"Ultimately , I think that you need to use your good judgement and help us create some rule of proportions about how television impacts our children and our grandchildren, some rule of proportion about violence, and a willingness to ask a basic gut question — is this good for the kids, or does it just sell product."

It's pretty clear the little *Clockwork Orange* kids would have kicked your basic gut and said loud and clear they were there to sell product. And to say it sucked.

In mid September it was announced that Paramount Communications would be attempting a merge with Viacom, the owners of MTV and *Beavis and Butt-Head*. *Advertising Age* reported on September 27th that the new company planned to introduce eleven interactive video games, including several based on "pop culture phenomenon" Beavis and Butt-Head. Do you smell movie deal next? WNYW-TV's *Good Day* reported that "Beavis and Butt-Head" were the property that drove Paramount into a deal with Viacom rather than the rival bid from Barry Diller's QVC.

On September 29th David Letterman flattered guest Jerry Lewis by comparing him to Beavis and Butt-Head, telling him there was a "purity of intent" there which they never deviated from. He also featured the little devils in cartoon form on subsequent shows and Dave even played the part of Beavis (or possibly Butt-Head) in a skit.

That same day *The Los Angeles Times* printed a smuggled photograph, filched by a film processing shop employee, showing media grand old man Alistair Cooke resplendent in a Beavis and Butt-Head fan club tee shirt. Cooke wasn't pleased, but hey, the truth always comes out.

October 3rd brought another long and thoughtful article in a major newspaper, this time *The Washington Post*. Twenty-year-old columnist Joe Mathews noted that he and his peers were members of a distinct and different generation from even their younger siblings. These youngsters considered twentysomethings to be "overindulged products of the late '60s and early '70s." Twentysomethings, he believed, worried about the deficit and the economy of this country, while the Beavis and Butt-Head generation, as he called them, "rejected ideals as impossible before they were potty trained." The Beavis and Butt-Head generation accepts fully the obvious fact that "the country is going down the toilet," and probably finds David Letterman "overly earnest."

Mathews' younger brother Peter, at 16, is an elder statesman of the Beavis and Butt-Head generation. Confirming the demographic picture of no hope for this generation, Peter agrees that the show is a "sad commentary on the state of today's teenager," but notes that this generation "is beyond expressing sentiment. It's powerless to do anything but laugh at itself." This generation has no luxuries, not even illusions about itself. As Peter says, "You can't be profound about anything as realistic as Beavis and Butt-Head."

This generational gap is also the one between Bart Simpson and our tykes. Bart is a symbol of adolescent rebellion. Throughout his run-ins with parents and his school Principal he is, "as smart as he is tough." Beavis and Butt-Head's fans celebrate them for their "idiocy." And if you think about it, this makes sense. If you cannot be rewarded for being smart, because there's nothing to reward you with, then why not protest by being as violently, angrily stupid and destructive as possible?

From there Mathews goes to the more essential issue, which is that most of "the age group assimilates the antics of Beavis and Butt-Head without much critical thought." Throughout the article he notes that when not commenting in a crude horny and sexist way about a woman's anatomy or disparaging a video the twosome will "do something terribly cruel to an animal."

He consulted Greg Feldmeth, who is a long-time teacher and school administrator in Southern California who has become an expert on Beavis and Butt-Head out of necessity. His school is over-run with Beavis and Butt-Head vibes in school assemblies, snickers in the hallways, and lunch time chatter. He says that, "The word fanatic could aptly describe quite a few kids he knows between the ages of 10 and 15."

Feldmeth's response is two-fold and contradictory. On the one hand he notes that his generation watched Wile E. Coyote, no slouch in the violence department, yet Western Civilization survived. Now he doesn't see it threatened by these two pimple heads. On the other hand, he can't quite bring himself to let his eight-year-old son watch *Beavis* in the house, though he lets him watch it at friends' houses. In his own house it's just "a forbidden thing." Does this sound like a man at ease with a popular phenomenon?

Mathews concludes that the young are already corrupted and that Beavis and Butt-Head won't do it to them. But he cites statistics, such as a survey of the Little League World Series players, where seventy percent of the twelve-year-olds named Beavis and Butt-Head as their favorite cartoon. With this in mind he can only conclude that sociologists, politicians, "anyone with an interest in the future of American society" need not look far to see the face of the twenty-first century. Its "founding principle will be nihilism. Rampant disregard for other living things will be in. Taking responsibility for one's actions will be out."

But stupidity does have its consequences. In one episode the terrible tots wandered onto a rifle range, shot down a passenger jet while target shooting, and couldn't figure out how to open the airplane's escape door, thereby leaving women and children to burn inside. But then, we all know how Beavis does love to watch things burn.

On October 6th, the American Psychological Association published a study showing that there are five to six violent acts during prime time TV daily. That day, a child took his Ninja Turtle sword and badly beat another child, following exactly what he'd seen in the cartoon "Teen Age Mutant Ninja Turtles."

On October 8th, in Moraine, Ohio, Austin Messner, age five, set his bed on fire while playing with a cigarette lighter. The boy, his mother and his mother's boyfriend escaped the trailer home; his sister Jessica, 2, died in the blaze.

Local fire brigade chief Howard Sigler quoted the mother as saying that her son "had never played with matches or lighters prior to witnessing Beavis and Butt-Head and laughing about fire being fun." Sigler added that he would be calling fire prevention groups to join him in an appeal to MTV to stop broadcasting the show.

Stories the same day reported that Beavis and Butt-Head merchandise was flooding the stores: key-rings, watches, calendars, mugs. Neighbors of the Messner family, notably Sheila Bonar, said "The kid was a pyromaniac and the family did not even get cable." MTV issued a statement saying that they did not have all the facts, but would reevaluate the program.

The following day CNN covered the story

in greater detail. Mother Darcy Burk was maintaining her position that Beavis and Butt-Head were a contributory factor to her boy's actions. Neighbor Sheila Bonar placed blame once more on the boy himself: "He just had a fantasy with fires. I mean, he set everything on fire." MTV was quoted as saying that while still unaware of all the facts, "responsibly programming MTV" had "always been" and would "continue to be a top priority."

Wasn't that just the kind of response that the Secretary of Education wanted? See, light a fire under their trailer and even MTV's gut-reaction will provide the right answer to a tough question—even if it is whether their priority is what's good for the kids of America or what sells product. At this point their priority was to exercise damage control—which is understandable—while doing what they could to protect their hottest commodity.

A caller on CNN's call-in discussion segment on the story said that government policy with regard to violence on TV and children "really just assumes that parents are watching what their kids are doing. When parents are monitoring what their kids are doing, we don't have to worry about those kids. It's the kids who have parents who aren't really keeping a careful track of...them, that might present problems later."

Another caller said that kids came home from school, watched violence on TV and "they think this stuff is OK and it's fine to do." Therefore TV was promoting violence in that it gave kids the idea that "yes, it's OK to do this. It's fine if you set a house or something on fire."

On October 11th, schools in South Falls, South Dakota responded to the news story with a ban on all images of Beavis and Butt-Head anywhere on school property.

That day *Newsweek* came out with a cover and a feature story on the dynamic dwarves. First, the article noted that the dorky duo were not just descendants of Wayne and Garth, Bill and Ted, etc,. But also of a comic sensibility and era of American writing that began with Letterman's Stupid Pet Tricks, an era that is "ironic, self-aware, and profoundly interested in the inherent dumbness of the tube."

The article *Newsweek* noted that while Mike Judge himself was an original, out of Dallas, and when his producer needed to put together a team of writers for the show he called Letterman's head writer for suggestions. They drew on the same pool of people who came out of a good university, had worked on something like National Lampoon and spent way too many of their formative years watching TV. To them TV was both camp, because they were smart, and the defining "fabric of shared experience."

The article also confirmed and added a different spin to the demographic view of Beavis and Butt-Head's audience. One in five people who graduated from college between the years 1984 and 1990 now holds a job for which no degree is necessary. "If this is not a hard economic reality for a whole generation, it is a psychological reality." *What Beavis and Butt-Head* and *The Simpsons* or *Married with Children* do is to tap "the anxiety in the culture and play it back for laughs." And so Homer Simpson works in a nuclear power plant and Al Bundy in a shoe-store. Your work environment can kill you AND humiliate you. Overall, Beavis and Butt-Head's stupidity makes them "totems of an age of decline and nonachievement."

Susan Smith-Pinelo, 24, a college graduate and artist who works a day-job as a receptionist, says that her generation can relate to "this lunatic fringe of teenagers who have fallen out of society", because it's so easy to do. Also, "we like to laugh at them and say "I'm not a loser" [like they are].

So our loathsome tots serve a double purpose — both as confirmation of how hard the world is to get ahead in now, and as encouragement that however much of a screw-up you are, you're not as bad at life as they are.

Gwen Lipsky, MTV's vice president of research and planning, made some interesting observations about the initial screening of Beavis and Butt-Head's "Frog Baseball" short on a test audience. The test group was "both riveted and hysterical" from the moment they saw it. As soon as it was over they asked to see it again. Then, after seeing it, several of the test group members asked if they could buy the tape.

Mike Judge himself notes that back when he was "the most miserable, awkward kid around" he and his friends did set fires for fun, just to see how many they could get going at once. He himself is a "total animal lover." Even as he was drawing the first cartoon about frog baseball he kept the story board hidden from people. He didn't want to show it to anybody and wondered "why am I doing this?"

That kind of thing is what we call Zeitgeist, Mikey boy! Or, as your two fiendish progeny might say — Dude you were too dumb to stop.

And too inspired, too pumped up. Beavis and Butt-Head got a hold of you and you just couldn't shake 'em, couldja? Huh-huh, huh-huh, huh-huh.

Both Judge and his team were sensitive to recent criticism, notably after the incident of a cat found killed by a firecracker in Santa Cruz five days after a joke was made on the show about doing such a thing. (Judge stresses that neither Beavis nor Butt-Head ever actually DID it). That incident had brought Dick Zimmerman to start his campaign against the show, largely because he felt that, unlike violent cop shows where at least a loosely defined "good" triumphs over "evil", this show demonstrated a "total lack of redeemability." But this is what kids watch it for, after all.

But Judge noted that the cat episode would not air again, and that three other episodes had been pulled from circulation. The show would be "considerably softened" in the new season. He conceded that the sniffing paint thinner episode — "we probably shouldn't have done," but added that at the time he thought the show was going on at eleven and "no-one's ever going to see it." He stated that he thought the show should only run at eleven, and that it had been toned down.

The issue of parental guidance, which would be at the heart of the ensuing debate, was also mentioned. Beavis and Butt-Head are characters totally out of the context of a nuclear family. Confronted with an image of a family dinner, their response is "Why's that guy eating dinner with those old folks?" Real kids supposedly have parents to monitor what they watch *and* what they do. President Clinton, the article notes, watches "American Gladiators" with his daughter. Presumably he doesn't let her beat-up office worker weenies.

However, what the article didn't say — and what Darcy Burk found in Ohio, is that most kids are not supervised most of the time. In this era of fractured nuclear families and one-parent families, with parent often out at their jobs, parental supervision of children's viewing and children's activities is not easily done.

John Leland, Senior Editor of *Newsweek*, concurred with Judge that the show should not air so early in the evening. MTV released a statement saying they would reexamine the show.

On October 12th, *The Star Tribune* ran a story on television violence and parental responsibility. The parents interviewed were activists in a campaign called "Turn Off the Violence," launched three years earlier by citizens of Minnesota. This campaign coincided with a Violence-Free Minnesota Week called by Governor Arne Carlson which would peak that Thursday with thousands of Minnesotans being asked to participate in "Turn Off the Violence Night."

The campaign had been mimicked in Louisville, Kentucky and San Diego, California, among other cities. Minnesota Attorney General Hubert Humphrey III declared: "We need to change how we view television...Like it or not we have to become responsible for the type of television we allow in our homes."

Parents quoted in the story listed several programs, among them *The Simpsons*, which were off-limits to their children. Beavis and Butt-Head are definitely considered off-limits.

That same day TV reports quoted Shelley Hettleman of Parent Action as saying that Beavis and Butt-Head were sending the wrong message to kids. Reports also noted that merchandisers were cashing in on the massive jump in sales of Beavis and Butt-Head items generated by the media attention.

On October 18th, Dick Zimmerman appeared on national TV advocating: parental control of TV watching by children, the taking of *Beavis and Butt-Head* off the air and greater community involvement if parental responsibility is not effective. California based super-squeezable doll makers reported a deal signed with MTV to manufacture Beavis and Butt-Head soft-sculpt dolls retailing for $10 as well as designer mugs and key-chains. *The New York Times* listed Beavis and Butt-Head getting their own show in their list of the years' "Moments of (Abundant) Nastiness."

Meanwhile, Moraine Fire Chief Sigler reiterated that the Messner boy was "obsessed" with Beavis and Butt-Head and always acted out what he saw on the show. A fire department in Austin, Texas held meetings educating school children about the dangers of fire, saying this was necessary to fight the influence of the cartoon show.

Mike Littrel, Austin Fire Investigator, explained on TV that several young arson suspects said that they'd seen the show *on* TV *and* "became inspired." Monica Givens, a 16-year-old Austen local, said the two boys who set the fire were "just using Beavis and Butt-Head as an excuse."

In another Ohio town, two girls watched the show and said they saw the dunces use a lighter and aerosol can to blow Beavis's head off. They tried it themselves and set their home on fire. MTV put out a statement that they would delete all future references to fire in the show.

On October 19th, MTV announced that Beavis and Butt-Head would no longer be screened at 7 pm; the two daily shows would screen back to back at 10:30 and 11:00 pm.

News reports quoted child psychologist Lawrence Balter as saying that the combination of adolescent pressures with a feeling of invulnerability was a "lethal combination."

The Chicago Tribune ran a story asking what do Beavis and Butt-Head have in common with a Roman Catholic bishop. Apparently both use MTV to reach American youth. The church bought five thirty-second commercials, to be shown only in the Scranton, Pennsylvania area, to promote the priesthood. Huh-huh, huh-huh, huh-huh, cool!

It was announced that a Senate committee would be reviewing violence on television the following week.

At around the same time, Touchstone Pictures, producers of a movie called *The Program*, responded to an incident in which two drunk teenagers in Polk, Pennsylvania imitated a scene in the movie and lay in the middle of a busy road, resulting in one of them getting killed and the other left in critical condition. Touchstone decided to cut the scene from the movie. This incident and its response from Touchstone did not help create a mood in the country or the media that would be favorable to Beavis and Butt-Head, as the Senate committee started its deliberations.

In another unfortunate comparison, Barney the puppet dinosaur was the cause of Ohio lives saved rather than lost when, as a result of being instructed during this children's show to run and tell Mommy if there's a fire, little Danielle Suthel woke her sleeping parents and thus saved her family and home when she smelt smoke.

One voice in favor of the twosome was *The Houston Chronicle*'s Jeff Daniel, who not only did not "buy" blaming Beavis and Butt-Head for the Ohio boy's fire-starting but also recommended buying shares of stock in Acme Dynamite Co.

TV personality and former children's show host Soupy Sales weighed into the debate in *Newsday*, saying that while he deplored Beavis and Butt-Head and thought they should have been "yanked off the air, period" — not just slotted later at night, he generally believed in parental guidance:

"Why are they so stupid as to leave matches and lighters around when children live in the home?...We must watch what our children do...we must tell them what is right and what is wrong."

He went on to say that TV "like life" had good things and bad in it. A parent could not just switch the TV on and leave it as a babysitter. Parents had also to switch it off when appropriate. But, essentially, "don't blame TV for the world's ills." Soupy also said it is up to parents to supervise the development of their children and grandchildren. "Good children can provide some guidance but in the long run, it is our responsibility Soupy concluded."

In the opening day of the senate committee on television violence Attorney General Janet Reno was the leading witness. During the course of extensive testimony she read out children's letters to her about "scary TV," cited a Journal of the American Medical Association study which found that children witness about 10,000 violent acts via television by the end of elementary school, as well as a National Institute of Mental Health report linking TV violence not necessarily to real life violence but certainly to real life aggression. The Attorney General concluded:

"We're just fed up with excuses and hedging in the face of this epidemic of violence. We've heard people say, "We'll do something about it," and they haven't done something about it."

She added that television networks needed to make these changes themselves and that the amount of violent programming needed to be lowered substantially and now. The regulation of violence "is constitutionally permissible." To this Senator Paul Simon of Illinois added that patience was wearing thin on the issue of television violence, that television was in fact busily selling violence and that government could create regulations if the industry did not take care of itself.

Senator John Kerry of (Nebraska) addressed the hearing to ask if Beavis and Butt-Head are the best a civilized society can produce as entertainment on television. Senator John Danforth of Missouri addressed the hearing to say that "most people" knew that "something had gone crazy" on television. He then addressed the Attorney General about a possible method of regulating violence levels on TV and its legality:

Danforth: Let us say that a television station were required by law to report every month on how many violent deaths it showed on that channel during the previous month. There would be no constitutional problem with doing that...would there?

Reno: No, sir.

Two different pieces of legislation are making their way through the bowels of Congress even as we speak, designed to quell this raging beast, this veritable inferno of media violence. Senator Edward Hollings, chairman of the Senate Commerce Committee hearing on Television Violence is sponsoring a bill to prohibit "violent video programming" during the hours when kids are supposedly watching. What those hours are and when they end and begin is anybody's guess. Here is also legislation pending which would obligate the Federal Communications Commission to issue a quarterly "violence report card" which, much in the manner of Senator Danforth's suggestions above, would list violent acts per station and, presumably, provide ammunition for prudes and popular censors across the political spectrum.

One voice of reason spoke up at the hearing: Jack Valenti, President of the Motion Picture Association of America, suggested that while it was "clear that Congress and the public and all of us...are fed up with the madness...that stalks our streets," there was still no reason to forget that "there's much more to the collapse of the assumed normalities in our society than a television set."

Peggy Charen, quoted above, and founder of Action for Children's Television, the nation's leading advocate for more healthful programming for kids still came down on the side of caution: "We have to be very careful not to take concern for children as an excuse to do in certain kinds of speech."

Gael Davis of the National Council of Negro Women underlined the nature and importance of the inappropriate television programing in that in a nation of often as not one-parent families and certainly two income, two working parent families, "television has truly become our electronic baby-sitter" for a generation of latch-key kids. Hence what television shows is not just entertainment, it carries for these kids the authority of what caretaker says. The problem being that while much can be said about the medium with kids as a justification, it remains questionable that the maker of a film or television program can be legitimately held responsible for the acts of its audience, let alone the acts of a tiny proportion of that audience.

The whole argument of TV violence scarring and influencing kids OR adult is based on the hard evidence of TV schedules in say the 1960's. Back to back Westerns with staggering bodycounts of dead rustlers, gun-slingers and Indians never made headlines and somehow did not apparently lead either to violence or discussion of the effects of such viewing. These include "The Lone Ranger", "Cisco Kid", "Have Gun will Travel", "Rawhide" and endless others. If you add to these the legion of cops and robbers series, it is interesting to note that not one fatality was blamed on the effects of a weekly drama in all of the turbulent, restless years of the civil rights movement and The Vietnam war.

Another problem is the argument that suggests some violence is "justified" and has "redeeming values", such as beating the crap out of a TV criminals. Other violence is considered "senseless", presumably Beavis and Butt-Head throwing goldfish in the incinerator blowing up things for the joy of it.

No one looks for redeeming values on the increasingly violent TV news programs, with their live-action violent spectacles such as the one staged by the Attorney General herself against the Branch Davidians in Waco, Texas. This incident dominated the airwaves repeatedly with the same images of destruction rebroadcast over and over for weeks, with much greater emotional impact on viewers than a half-hour fictional cartoon.

In fact, one local news reporter explained on a Nickelodeon program on TV violence that the news coverage philosophy is often: "if it bleeds, it leads." This is why News shows generally send cameras ONLY to FATAL auto accidents and why newsbroadcasts may be said to have an aesthetic centered completely around violence with NO redeeming values. Furthermore, it's one thing to tell a child that the violent movie was just a story, it's another to explain why the real life images of murder and mutilation on the news will not happen to them. "I get scared," said one child quoted on the Nickelodeon program, "because it's going to happen to me." Try telling them the boogieman will go away when local news show feature him hourly and throughout the night.

There is also, if nothing else the question of who will decide what is too violent to watch and for whom. Within the Senate committee on television violence there was a spectrum of views. Senator Hollings was outraged by a slapstick and somewhat sugar coated bar-room brawl in the light weight, soft CBS sit-com *Love and War*. Senator Conrad Burns of Montana responded, chortling, "If you were raised in Montana, it didn't look too violent." There was barely a bottle broken, for gosh-sakes! Let alone real injuries.

Even in the Congress's own analysis, the proposed legislation is not going to do anything that will have a significant effect. As Kristian Van Hook, policy analyst for the House Telecommunications and Finance Subcommittee noted, "Our read is that with 500 channels and video on demand this is not going to be effective...It would only apply to broadcasters who don't have that much violent programming before 9 pm." This, again, is a result partly of Congress not knowing what they're talking about—trying to deal with an industry that consists of networks, cable, local channels, etc., as if they were all networks—as well as the simple fact that Congress isn't really trying to solve the problem but, as suggested previously, they are just trying to look good.

As George Gerbner, professor of Communications at University of Pennsylvania's Annenberg School and a leading expert on television violence explains in Mark Jurkowitz's article on the subject in *The Boston Phoenix*, "The bills that are now pending are politically productive, but not a solution." These are, after all, the same people who waited years before passing a family-leave bill, disinvested in the inner cities, and continue to refuse effective gun-control and effective job-programs. Facing a society in marked and perhaps irreversible decline, it's easy to cry "television" rather than try to solve overwhelming problems. The gentlemen of Congress are, in Jurkowitz's words, "seeking simplistic answers to complicated questions." He suggests the best case scenario is that none of this legislation will make it through the system and so someone will go back to the drawing board and try to look at the problem more broadly.

Outside of Congress and in another vein, *The Hartford Courant* was covering the TV programming issue indirectly by doing a piece in defense of Barney the purple puppet dinosaur. Mentioned in this analysis so far only because his warnings about smoke led one child to wake up and save her family from a fire, the doting Dino may well be a positive force in children's lives. In a story by Jon Lender, Dorothy and Jerome Singer (child-development experts from Yale University), are quoted as saying that *Barney and Friends,* the PBS show has "an atmosphere that is emotionally upbeat...and one that establishes a context of love, trust and mutual care." The experts further note that such an atmosphere is a very fine thing for viewing children, and that the recent fad of "Barney-bashing" (would we do such a thing? Heh, heh, heh, heh...) "reflects a cynical lack of awareness by some adults of the urgency with which infants and preschool children require consistent periods of exposure to expressions of love and comfort and a sense of security."

All of which, presumably, is not well served by bad-complexioned youths chasing a live cat with a fire-cracker. NOT, as Mike Judge will tell you, that his toon twins ever did that, they just talked about it. The experts continue: "Something very basic is being met here-a loving, caring, predictably benign presence for the child, once a role played by grandparents or uncles or aunts when extended families lived in close proximity, but now much less available because of family fractionalization and mobility."

Which takes us back to the TV as "babysitter" problem and whether such a role should really be placed upon it, or rather, whether the moral standards demanded of a baby-sitter can really be applied to a market force like television. (If nothing else, many baby-sitters are pot-smoking, fridge-raiding, liquor cabinet-looting, sexually active teens who leave stains on your couch when you come home.

Certainly Beavis and Butt-Head might say "who wants to hang out with the old dudes anyway?" Most rational adults would have to say, it's not the smartest thing in the world to have your child become accustomed to getting their emotional needs, no matter how infantile and basic, fulfilled by a box with glass on the front of it and marketing messages blurting out at them every twelve minutes.

The ABC News show *Nightline* also got in on the debate by covering the hearings and holding a discussion of the issues between several media experts. Financial Analyst Paul Marsh pointed out that Touchstone pulling "The Program" out of cinemas for re-editing in order to excise the lying-in-the-road scene was a relatively cheap measure, amounting to perhaps $1000 per print, far less than an appearance of inaction in the face of the deadly incident might have cost. Drama critic for the

New York Times, Frank Rich, pointed out that *The Program* was a failing movie in any event, so pulling the scene was good publicity rather than lost revenue. Had the movie in question been, for example, the box office smash *The Fugitive*, whose scene of Harrison Ford jumping off a dam into raging water might just as easily have been imitated by drunken teens, the issue of re-calling a thousand movie prints might have been viewed differently.

Children's TV activist Peggy Charen took another tack, pointing out to the *Nightline* audience that the industry's haste to comply to criticism, be it MTV yanking *Beavis and Butt-Head* from the 7 pm slot or Touchstone re-cutting *The Program*, might send the wrong message:

"Historically the industry has liked to say, It's not our fault, it's a drama, it's free speech and by responding so fast they've run the risk...of looking like they were doing something wrong in the first place."

Michael Medved of TV's *Sneak Previews* took the view that the real problem was not the infinitesimally small number of people actually dumb enough to imitate what they saw on the screen, large or small, but rather "the influence on all the rest of us" in that movies and television now largely determined standards of "normal" behavior in America, increasingly defining not only "the kind of behavior that's accepted, but the kind of behavior that's expected."

Nightline's presenter Cokie Roberts retorted that we're in a lot of trouble "if normal behavior is what you're seeing on Beavis and Butt-Head." Media watcher Dick Wolf added that in any event there was always going to be material dangerous to some small portion of your audience and that this did not mean we needed "Big Brotherism" to protect the rest of the population from certain stories.

Frank Rich, then cited the historical comparison of his own childhood and the TV show *Superman,* and the reaction of a number of kids who jumped out of windows thinking they could fly. He concludes: "It would have been a tragedy for American culture if *Superman* had been censored by Big Brother."

(For you dudes out there too cool to read: "Big Brother" was the dictator type in George Orwell's novel *1984*; in that vision of the future every room had a TV in it, and every TV had a camera inside it, and behind every camera was a wire letting Big Brother know *exactly* what you were doing...(Sucks, don't it?)

Michael Medved responded that movies did influence people, not through these few incidents of copy-cat violence but through the "constant accumulation" of this material and the message that violence solves problems.

Dick Wolf, echoing some of the legislation in process, proposed a moratorium on violence on TV, every afternoon from 2:30 to 5:30, when kids were coming home from school. "Wouldn't it be wonderful if there were...no violent promos for movies,...no violent news images. Your kids could go home, and for that three hours a day...there would be no gunplay...no violence?"

As the show went to commercials figures ran across the screen from the Center for Media and Public Affairs, listing accuracies of TV violence in an average day:

> Serious Assaults 389
> Gun usage 362
> Punching 273
> Pushing/Dragging 272
> Property Damage 95

Fires were not mentioned specifically, nor Beavis and Butt-Head's own totals out of that glorious roll-call. But our boys surely were included, bless their little cartoon animated hearts.

After the break Dick Wolf suggested that violence had also been diminishing as an element in TV through market forces because "taste has changed" and that "television is the most perfect market society ever promulgated... As soon as a show loses viewership, the sponsors don't come and it's cancelled.

Cokie Roberts countered that the most violent shows of all according to experts were Saturday morning cartoons and, in any case, "are little children really a perfect market force?"

This led the panel to discuss *"Beavis and Butt-Head,"* with *The New York Times'* Frank Rich coming down firmly on the side of the dynamic dim-wits.

Frank Rich: "Who sets these standards? I have young sons who are basically pre-teen. They watch Beavis and Butt-Head. They would never think of setting anything on fire."

Asked how he felt about them watching such stuff, he said "Fine. I feel it's often a witty show" and concluded that their behavior was "determined by their home environment."

Discussion finally came down to how you could enforce standards, if any. If a producer could be sued as a result of someone imitating an action included in a television drama or a movie, could the public not also sue the news agencies and programs "because a story that was run caused a civil disturbance in which they were injured?"

Michael Medved brought the discussion to an appropriate close with his observation that it was not a case of parents wishing to abdicate responsibility to TV or to government, nor that they could not fight against the negative messages in the media:

"But why should we have to work so hard to try? Why can't there be a little more respect for the values parents want to pass to their own kids?"

A question Beavis might answer by saying "Because those values suck." And Butt-Head might concur: "Not cool."

P.S. Don't forget to turn off the stove. Or, you know, BOOM! Huh-huh, huh-huh.

CONCLUSION

by I.E.M.

If *Beavis and Butt-Head* were to go off the air in a year or so, it would still be long remembered as a significant mirror held up to American society and culture at the end of the twentieth century. Those who dismiss the show as infantile and crude are missing the point, but those who don't question these qualities in the medium are not paying enough attention to why we have to be the way we are.

This bravely experimental show has forced us to look at the sociopathic, pyromaniacal kid in the arrested human condition. These unthinking creeps have forced us to think about many of the significant issues that were raised in this book, one of them being the limits of free expression in the mass media. And, like the dimwits or not, the point can be made that this show is the most uniquely American program now on television.

Beavis and Butt-Head show no signs of letting up. On the contrary, the toon teen titans are going well beyond coffee cups and talking dolls that are helping them "Uh, heh, heh, heh" all the way to the bank. *New York Post* columnist Linda Stasi reports that a Beavis and Butt-Head book *(Tips On Dating),* an album (including a version of "I Got You Babe" with Cher), and a major motion picture are all in the works.

Is Mike Judge overreaching here? Probably not. Given the attention span of his average fan, he'd better strike now and not worry about oversaturation. If the boys stick with us for a few years, they might even grow with and carry their audience — the way The Beatles carried their generation from hand holding to social and cosmic consciousness.

Millions of their fans would like to see the B and B boys get into college, date girls, get jobs and confront their parents. If the show gets big enough it could outgrow its commercial function for the music industry.

The layered satire that appeals to postgrads as well as junior high kids could continue to grow in complexity and give us a fresh critical voice on many topics more important than the latest video that either "sucks" or is "cool". If this never happens, we'll understand. Beavis, Butt-Head and the rest of America never want to grow up.